instant manager
taking control of work and life

chartered
management
institute

inspiring leaders

overcoming
INFORMATION
OVERLOAD

TINA KONSTANT
& MORRIS TAYLOR

HODDER
EDUCATION

E LIVRE UK

The publisher has used its best endeavours to ensure that the URLs for external websites referred to in this book are correct and active at the time of going to press. However, the publisher and the author have no responsibility for the websites and can make no guarantee that a site will remain live or that the content will remain relevant, decent or appropriate.

Orders: Please contact Bookpoint Ltd, 130 Milton Park, Abingdon, Oxon OX14 4SB. Telephone: (44) 01235 827720, Fax: (44) 01235 400454. Lines are open from 9.00 to 5.00, Monday to Saturday, with a 24-hour message answering service. You can also order through our website www.hoddereducation.co.uk.

British Library Cataloguing in Publication Data
A catalogue record for this title is available from the British Library.

ISBN: 978 0340 959 022

First published   2008
Impression number   10 9 8 7 6 5 4 3 2
Year   2012 2011 2010 2009 2008

Typeset by Transet Limited, Coventry, England.
Printed in Great Britain for Hodder Education, part of Hachette Livre UK, 338 Euston Road, London NW1 3BH by Cox & Wyman Ltd, Reading, Berkshire.

Hachette Livre UK's policy is to use papers that are natural, renewable and recyclable products and made from wood grown in sustainable forests. The logging and manufacturing processes are expected to conform to the environmental regulations of the country of origin.

The Chartered
Management Institute

chartered

management

institute

inspiring leaders

The Chartered Management Institute is the only chartered professional body that is dedicated to management and leadership. We are committed to raising the performance of business by championing management.

We represent 71,000 individual managers and have 450 corporate members. Within the Institute there are also a number of distinct specialisms, including the Institute of Business Consulting and Women in Management Network.

We exist to help managers tackle the management challenges they face on a daily basis by raising the standard of management in the UK. We are here to help individuals become better managers and companies develop better managers.

We do this through a wide range of products and services, from practical management checklists to tailored training and qualifications. We produce research on the latest 'hot' management issues, provide a vast array of useful information through our online management information centre, as well as offering consultancy services and career information.

You can access these resources 'off the shelf' or we can provide solutions just for you. Our range of products and services is designed to ensure companies and managers develop their potential and excel. Whether you are at the start of your career or a proven performer in the boardroom, we have something for you.

We engage policy makers and opinion formers and, as the leading authority on management, we are regularly consulted on a range of management issues. Through our in-depth research and regular policy surveys of members, we have a deep understanding of the latest management trends.

For more information visit our website **www.managers.org.uk** or call us on **01536 207307**.

Chartered Manager

Transform the way you work

The Chartered Management Institute's Chartered Manager award is the ultimate accolade for practising professional managers. Designed to transform the way you think about your work and how you add value to your organisation, it is based on demonstrating measurable impact.

This unique award proves your ability to make a real difference in the workplace.

Chartered Manager focuses on the six vital business skills of:

- Leading people
- Managing change
- Meeting customer needs
- Managing information and knowledge
- Managing activities and resources
- Managing yourself

Transform your organisation

There is a clear and well-established link between good management and improved organisational performance. Recognising this, the Chartered Manager scheme requires individuals to demonstrate how they are applying their leadership and change management skills to make significant impact within their organisation.

Transform your career

Whatever career stage a manager is at Chartered Manager will set them apart. Chartered Manager has proven to be a stimulus to career progression, either via recognition by their current employer or through the motivation to move on to more challenging roles with new employers.

But don't take just our word for it ...

Chartered Manager has transformed the careers and organisations of managers in all sectors.

- *'Being a Chartered Manager was one of the main contributing factors which led to my recent promotion.'*
  Lloyd Ross, Programme Delivery Manager, British Nuclear Fuels

- *'I am quite sure that a part of the reason for my success in achieving my appointment was due to my Chartered Manager award which provided excellent, independent evidence that I was a high quality manager.'*
  Donaree Marshall, Head of Programme Management Office, Water Service, Belfast

- *'The whole process has been very positive, giving me confidence in my strengths as a manager but also helping me to identify the areas of my skills that I want to develop. I am delighted and proud to have the accolade of Chartered Manager.'*
  Allen Hudson, School Support Services Manager, Dudley Metropolitan County Council

- *'As we are in a time of profound change, I believe that I have, as a result of my change management skills, been able to provide leadership to my staff. Indeed, I took over three teams and carefully built an integrated team, which is beginning to perform really well. I believe that the process I went through to gain Chartered Manager status assisted me in achieving this and consequently was of considerable benefit to my organisation.'*
  George Smart, SPO and D/Head of Resettlement, HM Prison Swaleside

To find out more or to request further information please visit our website **www.managers.org.uk/cmgr** or call us on **01536 207429**.

Contents

CHAPTER 03

CHAPTER 04

CHAPTER 05

CHAPTER 06

HOW DO YOU DEAL WITH VERBAL OVERLOAD? 103

CHAPTER 07

HOW DO YOU AVOID OVERLOADING OTHER PEOPLE?   117

CHAPTER 08

CHAPTER 09

Preface

Overload can come from a number of sources and, while it affects every individual differently, the root cause is the same for everyone: the shift in perspective from being in control to being in chaos.

This book can help if you:

- have more work than time
- are reluctant to speed-read in case vital information is missed
- regularly deal with awkward, dull or technical information
- have a permanently full in-tray
- work, study and run a home
- feel overwhelmed with personal and business information
- are so busy that you forget important events or details
- want practical strategies for managing information.

Getting the most out of this book

Most adults, especially working parents, have at some time become overwhelmed with information. It's difficult to avoid.

Many people believe that the cure is to 'get busy'. However, the more you busy yourself, the more out of control you're likely to feel unless the 'busyness' is effective.

To make sure you get the most out of this book and ensure the 'busyness' of reading it is effective, read Chapter 5 – How do I manage written information? – first. Once you've read that chapter you can use smart reading strategies to help you process this material, and any other written material quickly and efficiently.

By reading Chapter 5 first you might also realise that, sometimes, the most important information you need isn't at the top of the pile, in the first chapter or the loudest, i.e. the phone. The most important information you need is the answer to this: 'What specific information do you need that will have the greatest impact on what you are doing?'

Chapter 5 and back again ...

The five steps explained in Chapter 5 will help you clarify your purpose, scan the material for what you specifically need and take an overview of the contents. This will allow you to determine what you need and what you don't. Finally, it will increase your ability to concentrate on what you have chosen to read.

Information is unlimited but our ability to manage it is not

When you try to use too much information at once the information begins to manage you. But information is only part of the issue. Problems start when people loading you with information also start to manage you. That's when you begin to lose control. It's then that, as an emergency measure, you have to adopt the 80/20 rule and identify the 20 per cent of what you do that's giving you 80 per cent of your results, and ditch the 80 per cent overload that's only producing 20 per cent of your results.

In a book as wide-ranging as this, it is inevitable that it incorporates some personal views and includes things that work for the authors. As you read this book and develop your skill to overcome information overload you will find additional strategies, not included in this book, that will work for you.

What is information overload and how do you know if you have it?

Information overload is an easy trap to fall into because on the surface, it seems like the problem comes from the world around you: people overload you; work overloads you; family overloads you; the media, the Internet and advertising overload you. It's not your fault.

On closer inspection, all the world is offering you is information. What you do with that information is what determines how overloaded you are. So before we begin, it's important to define exactly what information overload is.

What is information overload?

Overload is a matter of perspective. The severity is determined by your perception of the consequences of not dealing with excess information. Some people deal with uncontrolled information (even if the consequences of ignoring it seem severe) because they have a higher panic threshold than others.

Information overload doesn't happen in isolation. If your life is in control then you will be able to manage vast amounts of new, unexpected, conflicting or challenging information. It will seem to you that your mind is open and able to cope with anything new – you are happy, calm and in control. If however, your life takes a turn and one area becomes uncontrolled – family, marriage, relationships, money – your ability to *cope* with new information will be suddenly and dramatically reduced.

In the Japanese martial art of aikido, you learn that when someone grabs you by the wrist that it is only that part of you that they control. You can still move the rest of your body. Treat information in the same way.

The small part of your life that seems out of control can momentarily blind you to the real scale of your problem. The trouble is, when you experience the emotional feelings that often go with overload, the pieces of information become attached to those feelings along with the potential of too many overbearing consequences. If you gain perspective over the problem and take control, your perception will change and so will your environment.

The purpose of information

How we perceive information and what we decide to do with it determines whether our lives are run by it or whether we are in control. Information can strengthen and secure our position at work. At home, information allows our family to control their lives. Information can also lead to independent wealth. We can have access to all the information the world has to offer, but if we don't use it appropriately, it becomes overload.

If you feel overloaded with information, you are taking in too much, attaching too much importance to it or doing too little with it. It is better to do a lot with a small amount of information than to try to move forward on the inconsequential or the irrelevant, which can lead to the symptoms of overload.

The symptoms of information overload

Apparent memory difficulties: Small things slip your mind. You get through the day but can't remember, at the end of the day, what you did at the beginning of it. You can't remember the names of people you have just met. You have difficulty recalling details, facts and figures. You have conversations during which you tend to 'zone out' and you find yourself unable to contribute because you literally didn't hear or take in what anyone was saying.

Easily distracted: You find yourself daydreaming or going blank for periods of time. Your mind leaps from one subject to another with no apparent connection between the subjects. You start sentences and conversations but don't finish them. You start projects and tasks but don't finish them. Everything gets your attention and you find it difficult to concentrate for long periods of time.

Worry: Your time may be taken up with concerns and fears about what you might be missing or what you should be doing. You worry about what other people are doing and about how what you're not doing will affect them. You might also worry about what people think of your competence or your ability to do your job. You might become uncomfortable during meetings because you feel you're behind everyone else and are paranoid that everyone knows.

Over-compensation: Even though you know you can't keep up you might take on even more in the belief you will give the illusion of being in control. Trouble is, if you're not in control, the more you take on, the less you can do. To hide that you're in trouble you might talk a lot but deliver little, especially if the tasks are either difficult or outside your skill range. Instead of halting the situation and allowing a re-evaluation, you might start a series of conversations intended to delay delivery. This shares the load by passing information (or non-information) to others so that it becomes impossible for you to complete the task because 'you're waiting for Joe Doe to get back to you'. You've created gateways so that others have to do non-work before you can do the real work. This widely used tactic shifts blame on to all the other people you pulled into those conversations. Effectively, what you say is: 'I couldn't do this task because Joe Doe didn't get back to me with this particular infinitesimal piece of useless information.' By then those around you are so confused that they've forgotten the original scope of the job, it goes beyond what they feel they should be doing or gets handed off to someone else.

Stress: This leads to over-eating, under-eating, too much sleep, too little sleep, extremes of everything and is one of the key indicators of overload. This is covered in more detail in Chapter 2.

Procrastination: When you have so much to do that you can't decide what to do, you will do nothing. Many people wait until a situation becomes critical. They deal with what is urgent, when it's urgent, and only because it's urgent. As well as adding to stress, procrastination can lead to the overwhelming feeling of being out of control. Procrastinators forget that they're in a perpetual state of emergency because they've sat for days or weeks in a state of worry and fear. If they had taken action sooner, they would not have to deal with any emergency and they probably wouldn't be overloaded. Procrastination is not only a symptom of overload, it is one of the direct causes. However, not all procrastination is bad. Sometimes it's a signal from your brain that you've missed something important and you shouldn't take another step until you've identified it and dealt with it.

Frozen: This happens when you are feeling so overloaded you can't cope. When you reach this stage you become incapable of doing anything. You don't think, you don't act, you don't respond to what's going on around you. You feel numb and apparently oblivious to the consequences of your inaction. Despite the urgency you not only do nothing but you feel nothing. You pass the load to someone else who may have noticed that you're overloaded. If no one has noticed, they soon will when a deadline is missed. Regardless of the consequences, you will still have done nothing. The chain of warning signs looks like this:

Anatomy of information overload

1. **Life is good.** You're generous with your time and frequently say things like 'sure, I can do that' to any request. You're feeling good. The world is in order.
2. **Requests increase because you're a 'can-do' individual.** Information flows your way and you begin to notice a slight sense of unease. You ignore it but start avoiding certain people or certain topics of conversation.
3. **Work stacks up.** You notice that you don't open all your mail every day. E-mails stack up. Your mental attitude is still good: 'I'll catch up on Saturday. Kids can look after themselves. It'll only take an hour or so.'
4. Gradually, **weekends, evenings and holidays turn in to catch-up times.**
5. **A rift forms between professional and personal life.** You don't want your family and friends to suffer because you have a 'bit too much on your plate', so instead of spending a couple of hours catching up, you sneak time here and there to do what you have to do. You feel bad because you're not being totally honest with your family or with yourself. But you do what you have to do.
6. Instead of sneaking time at home, you decide you'd get a lot more done, a lot quicker, if you stayed at work a little longer. So you do. **Your hours extend.** First evenings, then Saturday morning, then all day Saturday.

7. **People around you are annoyed because 'you're always at work'.** You get annoyed because they're annoyed: 'I have to. I have no choice. It's my job.'

8. **Tension builds at home and in your social life.** You start to go to work to get away from it all. But you're tired and frustrated. Overload increases. Cracks show. Your behaviour changes. People at work notice that you're snappy, disorganised, late for meetings. Trouble is, you've said yes to so many people and projects that your commitments prevent you from backing out. You're in a moral catch-22: you said yes to be helpful and professional but your desire to continue to be helpful and professional is preventing you from regaining control over your environment.

9. **Your mind crosses a line and you shut down.** You step into your office after working all weekend and having had a fight at home. You open e-mails. Glance down at the stacked in-tray. There's another request from someone. It's not a big request. The deadline isn't that urgent. They probably wouldn't mind if you said 'no' (although they would be surprised because you've said 'yes' to everyone else).

10. **Information overload hits you square in the face.** You can't see wood for trees and you have bark embedded in your forehead to prove it. Suddenly, you're out of control and don't know what to do next.

What to do next

If you feel that your mind is about to collapse under the strain, step out of the 'overload' environment – home or office. This includes temporarily distancing yourself from anyone you think may be contributing to your feelings of overload – friends, family, colleagues.

Your initial reaction to this may be: 'I can't!! I have too much to do!! My family/colleagues need me!! I'm a mum/dad with responsibilities!! I can't just take time out!!' The alternative is to carry on as is.

Your don't have to take a week out of your life; just a few hours – maybe a day at most.

Take a clean, new notepad and a pen. Leave everything else behind: briefcase, bag and all the clutter you carry with you. Find a place where you can sit and think – teashop, park, anywhere. Take a little time to put what's going on around you in perspective by answering the following questions:

1. What part of your life is currently not working – work, money or family? Remember, we're dealing with information overload and not general life fixing. Focus only on work, family or money – three areas where overload tends to congregate.
2. Which part of your environment is the most cluttered – home, work or both?
3. Of the areas you've identified, which do you feel most emotional about? Where do you feel most angry, frustrated or sad? Many other factors can contribute to feelings of anger, frustration or sadness, so think only in terms of information overload. After you have information in control, and reduced the emotional effects of overload, other things may change too.
4. Once you've identified what overloads you, list all the people in that environment who contribute to that overload – friends, family, colleagues, bosses.
5. Next to each person's name, write down what you think their expectations of you are. What do your children expect? What does your boss expect? Your creditors? Your bank manager? Your colleagues? Don't take the easy way out and just say 'everything'. Break it down. Ask yourself what each person in your life *specifically* expects of you.

6. When you have that list for each person in your life, take the time to be honest and reasonable with yourself. Ask yourself what is genuine and what is self-inflicted. Are you the mental and physical store house for everyone's schedules? Does that work for you? Is it causing you to burn out? Is it possible for each person to be responsible for their own schedule? What would happen if they were? What if you weren't responsible for other people's lives? What if they took responsibility?

7. When you have your list of true and reasonable expectations (personal and professional), list all the information you're currently dealing with to satisfy each of those expectations: schedules, bills, banking, tasks, projects, deadlines.

You should now have a list of all the main people in your life. Those who, as well as contributing to your sense of wellbeing, may overload you, perhaps without intending to. Each person's expectations will be divided between what is real and what is self-inflicted. All your current tasks, deadlines and activities associated with each of those expectations should also be listed.

It's important that you're honest with and about yourself. Not being honest will mean that as you begin to untangle the overload, you'll be focusing on the wrong information. You might focus on your job where in fact, it's not that. It may be that monthly bills are actually causing the overload. If you focus only on your job, you'll feel pressure and just work harder (but not necessarily smarter) and not focus on the fact that your finances are in disarray – 'I'm working as hard as I can! What more can I do?' doesn't fly with credit cards and bank managers. Your greatest enemy is denial.

Now comes either the really easy part, or the truly difficult part – it all depends on what's on your list.

8. If you experience overload at work, at home and in your finances, prioritise them by determining which has the greatest consequence if ignored. Deal with that first. You won't be ignoring the other areas of your life. You'll just be dealing with the tough one first.

Working on trivia is okay if you are the only person affected by your overload. It makes you feel busy and, for a while, there are no great consequences. The real issues start when your overload affects the outside world – especially the world of finance, government, business colleagues, friends and family. When your overload makes those people unhappy, you will have a problem you can't ignore.

If your finances are in disarray, every envelope will fill you with dread. Your behaviour towards simple daily tasks will change. You won't answer phone calls. Won't open the mail. You refuse to acknowledge the problem. This is simple denial. But just because you're ignoring the situation, it doesn't mean anyone else is.

When information overload is a good excuse

Do you like to feel overloaded? Does it make you feel important? Do you secretly enjoy being the person in the office with so much to do that you have to come into the office at 6 a.m. and can only leave at 8 p.m? Does it make you feel indispensible? Do you care that people notice that you come in early and go home late? You are unlikely to admit this to anyone except yourself (and even that might not be possible) but do you find relief in being able to tell your family that you can't do certain things with them because you're too overloaded at work and you need to work late or work over the weekend in order to catch up? Do you use the 'too much to do' excuse to avoid things you don't want to do?

If so, you're doing one of two things:

- You're **consciously** making up overload so you can use it as an excuse to get out of doing what you don't want to do or being where you don't want to be.
- You're **unconsciously** making up overload so you can use it as an excuse to get out of doing what you don't want to do or being where you don't want to be.

Either way, you need to take the time to understand what you are trying to avoid and what damage you are doing to yourself, your family, your social life and your job by making yourself appear too busy to deal with the important stuff in your life.

If you don't, people will eventually stop asking you to join in. They will assume you are too busy and when you decide you need to rejoin the world, it might not be so easy.

How to deal with overload when it's not 'just in your head'

Sometimes overload is not just in your head. Sometimes it is very real and takes the form of paper, e-mails, books, deadlines, visual and auditory noise.

It is vital to keep a clear head and maintain perspective no matter how much apparent overload you're collapsing under. I say apparent, because you are the one who has decided you're overloaded. Other people may load you up with work and information, but you have flipped the mental switch from control to chaos.

In brief

The key to managing information overload is the following:

- Develop an attitude of control.
- Plan and organise yourself – not the world.
- Decide your purpose and the information you need to make it happen.
- Have access to the information you need rather than attempt to store and juggle it.
- Control the flow of information.
- Learn to say 'no' (to yourself and others).
- Take responsibility for your current workload.
- Share information that needs to be shared – don't be an overload martyr.
- Develop the personal habits that will prevent overload from ever being an issue again.
- Concentrate on one issue at a time.
- Work as efficiently as possible.
- Finish the job!

INSTANT TIP

Get perspective! Pondering and worrying will do nothing except make the problem bigger than it is. Stop. Step back. Assess the true dimensions of your overload issues. Then ACT.

02

How do you cope with stress caused by information overload?

As mentioned in the previous chapter, stress is one of the key indicators of information overload. Whether or not the overload is genuine, the stress symptoms will be real.

Clear your head when pressure is at its peak

There are thinking cells in your kidneys, liver, heart and gut that are identical to the cells that make up your brain. Your body is populated with thinking cells. As a result, gut feelings, butterflies in your stomach, prickles in your neck and heartfelt feelings are more than mere sensations. Your body is like a radar system, constantly picking up information from your environment. It's never overloaded. It delegates. It notices what's important and ignores the rest. When something requires your attention (impending danger for instance) your body gives you a combination of physical and emotional messages. These messages are sometimes in the form of a feeling or 'little voices' and are often ignored. Yet, as well as help you make the right decision, they can save your life.

The more you understand and trust your instincts (as opposed to reacting instinctively), the easier it will be to make clear and accurate decisions in difficult situations. The more in touch you are with your body, the easier it will be to understand the information it gives you.

This chapter will help you:

- be more sensitive to your instincts and take them into account when making decisions
- reduce stress
- respond more calmly to your environment
- increase health and wellbeing
- reduce internal conflict and panic in challenging situations.

These techniques take only a moment to do. The more you practise them the more benefit you will feel. You don't, however, have to practise them for long. Also, some strategies you will like, others you may not. Select the ones you prefer and use those. Learning to read your body is not like fine wine or food, if you don't like a particular technique, don't use it. You don't have to suffer to benefit.

Listen to your heart

Any time you feel stressed, overloaded or are faced with a difficult situation or decision:

1. Think about the decision or event or situation you want to handle.

2. Breathe and focus your attention on your feet, then your knees, then your hands. Notice any sensations in those areas.
3. Focus your attention on the area of your chest surrounding your heart.
4. Imagine what it would be like if you were able to breathe through your heart. We know you can't, so just *pretend*. Imagine if air did not pass through your mouth, nose and lungs, if that whole area was silent and instead, you could breathe, clearly and fully, directly with your heart.
5. After a while, recall a time you experienced true appreciation. Recall who was there, and what it felt like.
6. Recall that feeling and, when you have it back, go back to your heart.
7. Ask your heart how it would handle the situation or decision you are finding difficult.
8. Pay attention to the answer and notice any sensations, emotions or feelings.
9. Make a decision on what you are going to do next.

The above may take a few minutes the first time you try it. After you have done it a few times you can *begin* by breathing with your heart. It is one of the quickest ways of reducing stress in any situation.

Body watching (your own!)

The purpose here is to increase your awareness of your whole body: cells, muscles and blood flow. It is extremely relaxing and helps get rid of aches and pains and clear your mind.

1. Choose a place where you feel safe and secure and where you won't be disturbed.
2. Sit comfortably or lie down.

3. Imagine you can see inside your body, either from the inside or from the outside (experiment to find out which you prefer at different times).

4. Go through your body starting from the surface and work your way into the centre of your body. Imagine being inside your skin. What does the layer between your skin and muscle look, feel or sound like? Explore the skin all over your body from your toes to your scalp. Then go deeper and explore your muscle fibre. What colour are your muscles? What is the texture? What is attached to your muscle? How fast or slowly are your muscles moving? Is there a space between your muscles or are they tightly packed together? Next, explore your veins and other blood vessels. What colour is your blood? Is it really only red or are there other colours in there too? Are the walls of your veins and vessels smooth or rough? Once you have explored every inch of vein or vessel, explore your bones. Are they hard all over or are there tender soft areas? Are they moist or dry? What joins them? What flows inside them? How are they attached to your muscles? Finally, explore your organs. Are they working quickly or slowly, what is going in and coming out of them? Are they comfortable or not? What kind of energy flow is there in your body? Is there enough water? Look at every part of your body.

5. After you have explored your whole body, ask if there is anything you can do to make it healthier.

6. Listen to the response, then act on it.

If you do this regularly, you may notice that small aches and pains disappear. Also, if something really is wrong, you will have a better chance of noticing it sooner because you will be in touch with your body and general health condition. Most important, it pulls your mind out of the frustrations you might be experiencing and allows you to centre, slow and focus your thinking on something positive.

Use your senses

This needs two people. It is wonderful to do with children.

Use a blindfold to inhibit vision. The blindfolded person will be presented with a variety of stimuli – touch, sound, taste or smell. The purpose is to encourage the blindfolded person to describe what they hear, smell, taste or feel by describing the *pictures* they see in their heads when they are presented with the stimulus. If you put their hand on a warm radiator for instance, they cannot simply say, 'it's warm'. Encourage them to describe what warm might look like if they turned it into a picture. If they cannot find a picture immediately, start at the edge, asking them to describe what colour it might be, then what shape, then any movement and gradually, from the images, a picture of the feeling will emerge.

The key here is *safety* and *permission*. As soon as someone puts a blindfold on they trust you. Don't present them with anything alive (even if it's a family pet) or anything that might harm or startle them (for example, anything too hot or too cold). The more relaxed the blindfolded person is, the easier it will be to generate visual images. And remember, it'll be your turn next!

Surround awareness

This also needs two people. The implications of it go beyond simply being aware of what is going on around you. Have you ever gone to an interview or met someone new and noticed that you move around in your chair until you are comfortable? Or how someone can be standing next to you and you just feel uncomfortable for no obvious reason yet as soon as they (or you) move, even just a little, the discomfort eases?

Most people are sensitive in one way or another to *some* of their immediate space. Some don't like anyone standing behind them; others don't notice it at all. My personal discomfort happens if I am standing in front of someone's desk when they are sitting behind it. It feels like I'm getting my homework marked by a teacher who is being too liberal with a red pen. If you are aware of where you are most or least comfortable in your personal space, you will be able to position yourself (say at a meeting or interview) so that you feel safe and comfortable. If you are with someone who looks uncomfortable, be aware that you might be sitting in one of his or her sensitive spaces.

1. Sit in a chair or stool in the middle of a room.
2. Have someone you trust stand approximately two metres in front of you.
3. Eyes open or closed, ask your partner to walk slowly around you in a circle.
4. Notice the sensations in your body, notice changes in your breathing. If you begin to feel uncomfortable, ask your partner to stop moving, notice their location, then ask them to move on, each time noticing where they are standing when you feel most or least comfortable.
5. After you have done it once, experiment with distances and the combinations of you and your partner sitting and standing. Ask the person you are working with to walk a circle around you only one or a half metre in diameter and then again at perhaps three or four metres.
6. Notice any differences when you try this with someone you don't know so well.

A good extension to this experiment is to check your surroundings in public places. Next time you are having lunch or coffee somewhere, close your eyes and mentally imagine walking around your body. Notice where you feel any discomfort. Then, open your eyes and look around the room. What is in the places in the room where you felt uncomfortable?

Ten tips on minding your body

1. Be as healthy as you can. The more you take responsibility for your body the less interference you will get from aches and pains.
2. Psychological pain caused by overload can become physical pain. Pain is information. Pay attention to it.
3. Trust your instincts, they are mostly right.
4. Spend at least a few moments each day reading your body.
5. Relax!
6. Trust the instincts of others.
7. Get plenty of quality sleep and exercise.
8. Be aware of your surroundings and the effects of the location of yourself and others.
9. Slow down. Your body sometimes takes time to deliver the message.
10. When making decisions, ask your body first.

Regain your perspective

Once you have managed your stress, maintain your wellbeing by regaining your perspective. The world is what it is: madness, aggression, peace, harmony, contradictions, differences and overload. It is your *perception* that determines whether it is chaos and disorder or sense and order. Think of a busy airport, people rushing everywhere, bumping and complaining, looking lost and bewildered. It's hot, your bags are heavy, everything is in chaos. You become tense and before you know it, you would rather you weren't taking any trip to any exotic island. Step back for a second. Take a look at the scene. Don't try to push and shove your way through people. Take your time, breathe and relax. Take the events for what they are. Just a busy airport. Your mood begins to change, people seem to smile more. Anticipation replaces frustration. In a moment, the chaos becomes excitement and fun. Airports are start points of adventure. For the most part, they are exciting places. A change in perspective allows you to experience a different world, one free from anger, frustration, fear and debilitating tension.

Consider another example. Wars are fought because two sides have different views of who is right and who is wrong. People inflict the most horrific acts on each other believing they are perfectly justified and right in doing so. What is terrorism to one cultural viewpoint is the justified action of a 'freedom fighter' to another. How do you persuade one side to acknowledge and appreciate the sentiments of the other? Our perceptions are not only ingrained in our conscious thoughts but they are in our unconscious behaviours that come from generations of behaviour and belief.

Dealing with information in a calm, balanced state allows you to change some of your ingrained thinking. You have the opportunity to consider someone else's perspective before making a judgement. It also means that when stress and negative responses to a situation are simply making matters worse you have the skills required to stop, slow down, change your perspective and see things in a more constructive light.

Practise perspective

This exercise can be done wherever you have some time to play – sitting at a bus stop, having a cup of tea somewhere or attending a meeting that is proving to be uninteresting! Notice an event or activity going on around you at the time. An event containing some tension works best: an argument between two people; a parent struggling with a moody child; a waiter managing a tricky customer – anything that has the potential of a less than positive ending. Imagine you were *part* of the event. How would you manage it? Next, imagine you were one of the people involved in the event, or a world leader or someone else entirely. How would you manage that event if you were someone else? Step into their shoes, think of what these different people would have to consider in responding to the event. What would you bring to the event that they could not?

Look for reasons why the event should or should not be taking place. Look for reasons why each person might be right or wrong. Look for justification for each person's actions. Look at the event from every perspective possible. Practise this often, play with it and then take it seriously when you are in a position of conflict.

Two important notes to remember:

- Although you might be able to appreciate another person's perspective, you don't have to agree.
- A person's actions *always, always, always* make perfect sense to them.

Respond to stress and change perspective on overload

Stress happens either when your situation outweighs your perceived ability to deal with it, or worse still, when you are overloaded without realising it. This perception will vary day to day, moment to moment. 'Perception' is the operative word. You might have no more to do on Tuesday than you had on Monday, but because your mood or environment is different, what you have to do might seem more than it really is, and the perception that you cannot cope will increase regardless of the reality of your current surroundings.

A thought experiment

Think of a busy main street you are familiar with. Imagine two people walking along that street. Both see the same street, same people, same events. A bus narrowly missing a cyclist, someone getting her bag snatched, a couple fighting, a child crying. As the couple walk down the street one will be tense and frustrated and the other will shrug and say, 'that's life'. The very next day, the same two people walk down the same street. This time, their reactions are reversed. The one who felt quite relaxed the day before notices exactly the same events and this time, is upset by them. The person who was agitated the day before doesn't respond at all.

Stress is created by the way you respond to a situation rather than the situation itself. In a potentially stressful environment, instead of focusing on how not to get stressed by it, focus on how you can deal with it and improve it.

A number of stressors can affect your ability to perceive the world in a calm, balanced way:

- **Environment** – noise, chaos and pollution
- **Social** – people, deadlines, financial problems
- **Physiological** – aches, pains, poor nutrition, lack of exercise

By far the most dominant and potentially damaging are:

- **Your own thoughts** – it is the *interpretations* that we place on a situation that generate stress. As Shakespeare says, 'There is nothing either good or bad, but thinking makes it so' (Hamlet).

Re-interpret stress

Break the routine

It is important you pay attention to the messages your body brings to your conscious awareness and that you act on that information. Your body is hormone driven and works on a cycle throughout the day. When you feel like you need a cup of tea or coffee, or you start yawning or making mistakes, your body is telling you it is time to stop and rest (see Ernest Rossi's book *The 20 Minute Break*). The longer you put off having a break, the more difficult it will be to get back to work after you finally decide to take one. If you have a lot to do, it is better to take plenty of little breaks and small snacks during the day rather than work through the whole morning, stop for a full lunch and then suffer in the afternoon.

Carrot or stick

One way to encourage yourself to keep your mind open and your perspectives clear is to reward yourself. If you work in a conventional environment you may not feel that you are fully recognised or rewarded for your efforts. Instead of waiting for a reward for your work to come from somewhere else, take responsibility for giving yourself a reward. At the beginning of the day determine the things you are going to accomplish and what your rewards will be (*not* sweets and sugars – this only rewards the taste buds!). Vary your rewards. Choose things that are good for you, things you really want: anything ranging from an evening in a steam room to a proper holiday for finishing a big project on time. Have plenty of reasons to treat yourself. You will feel happier, your motivation will increase and your stress levels will reduce.

Anti-ostrich policy

Maintain an anti-ostrich policy. Being open-minded and receptive to new ideas will make your day more creative and problem free. If you avoid sticking your head in the sand you will be aware of what is going on around you and on the look out for potential problems and their solutions. Potential problems only *become* real and unmanageable when they are ignored. Keep your head out of the sand and your mind open. When you no longer fear managing difficult issues, they won't seem so big. Fear of problems makes them worse. Treat problems for what they are – a series of events that you have to disentangle. Remember, however, the other extreme: 'hyper vigilance'. That can be just as damaging albeit in a different way.

Rid yourself of clutter and confusion

An environment you can and must control is your workspace. Every piece of paper on your desk will attract your attention several times a day. If each piece of paper had a deadline attached to it, you would have a desk full of alarm clocks sounding off every five minutes alerting you to the pressure you are under, interrupting your concentration, inducing chronic stress and causing long-term damage to your *capacity* to concentrate.

If you have a clear desk, your environment will look and feel in control. You may have a great deal to do but you will be able to tackle each task one at a time with a clear mind. The perception that your environment is out of control will diminish if it looks organised.

The 'three month' test

A delegate in one of my (*TK*) workshops had a novel method of dealing effectively with unread clutter. He would place everything that came onto his desk into one pile in a tray in the corner. If he needed it, he took it out of the pile and then placed it on top if he knew he would need it again. Gradually, all the paper work and documents that he did not need and did not have to read would work their way to the bottom of the pile. Then, every three months he would take the bottom half of the pile and, without going through it, throw it away.

His argument was that if he did not need it in three months he would not need it at all, and that if it really was important someone would have sent him another copy and the new copy would be in the top half of the pile.

He is very successful in business and since he adopted this strategy he has quartered the amount of reading he does because people know that if they want him to pay attention to something they must take the time to call him. As a result, his desk is always clear, so is his mind.

Your living space

This is not an exercise in Feng Shui, although Feng Shui is worth a look at. Your living space is a reflection of your mind and thinking processes. Look at your home. Compare the state of your home and the state of your mind.

If you are happy with your living space, if you love going home, if you feel calm and peaceful, creative and relaxed in your living space, then your living space is right for you. If, on the other hand, you spend most of your time out because every time you go home you are reminded of chores you don't want to do then it may be worth taking some time to organise and clear your space so that you can live in it, rather than use your creative ability to generate excuses on how to avoid it.

The space you live in should be the one place in the world where you can just 'be'. If you have a big, chaotic family make sure you have at least *one* space and one time that is yours.

Exercises to reduce stress and maintain perspective

Breathing

Although most of your brain cells would die without oxygen within three to five minutes, you can live a whole lifetime without breathing *properly* and not be aware of it. Your body uses your breathing as a signal to tell you when something is wrong; when you are feeling stressed or threatened you feel it in your breathing. When you are tired, you yawn to take in more air. When you are in a room with poor ventilation it doesn't take long before you feel uneasy, get a headache or feel tired. These signals should not be ignored.

Correct breathing relieves a number of symptoms including stiffness, tension, irritability, headaches, fatigue and depression. Poor breathing habits considerably impact your ability to monitor stress and respond positively to events around you.

Several breathing exercises that don't take long to do and that you can do in any environment will help reduce stress. These exercises are easy to learn. Practise a breathing exercise several times every day at the same time or in response to a regular occurrence. This will gradually become a routine and will help remind you that you have a choice when a situation gets out of hand.

Your body will soon learn to relax naturally, in a very few moments, when you are faced with a challenging situation that requires thought, an open mind and a shift in perspective.

This is a good breathing exercise if you don't want others around you to know you are doing it. At each in-breath make sure you are breathing into your abdomen rather than your chest. To check this (assuming you can't place your hands on your abdomen area to check whether it is moving or not), place your awareness around your waist and, as you breathe, you should feel a tightening around your clothing.

1. Exhale comfortably and take in a slow, deep breath and hold for the count of eight.
2. Slowly exhale.
3. Take three or four breaths like this and relax.
4. Accompany the breathing with a good stretch if you can.

If you have only a few minutes, this yoga breathing exercise is wonderful for relaxing and focusing.

1. Close your eyes for a few moments.
2. Place your right thumb on your right nostril and block it.
3. Breathe in deeply and slowly through your left nostril for six seconds.
4. Block both nostrils using your thumb and your middle finger and hold for six seconds.
5. Remove your thumb from your left nostril only and slowly exhale.
6. Pause for six seconds.
7. Then continue by breathing in through your left nostril, closing both, and exhaling through your right.
8. Continue to do this for as long as you feel comfortable.

If you are tired and you have much to do, this will help wake you up and increase alertness.

1. Stand or sit up straight.
2. Breathe abdominally.
3. Hold your breath for a count of six.
4. Purse your lips and blow out short bursts of air fairly forcefully until you have totally exhaled.
5. Breathe in deeply again and repeat the exercise several times.

Being present and in perspective

It is impossible (and undesirable) to be totally present and focused all the time. Imagination and creativity happens when your mind wanders beyond your present space and time. Sometimes, however, you need to be fully present and aware. This exercise will help you develop the necessary state of mind.

1. Sit or stand still for a moment.
2. First, close your eyes if you can and notice what you can hear. How many conversations can you make out? What are people saying? Can you hear any traffic? What is the furthest sound you can hear? What is the closest sound you can hear? What is the most familiar or the most foreign or unusual sound? What is the most or least pleasant sound? Describe every sound you can hear.
3. Next, notice what you can feel. How close are people to you? What does the floor feel like beneath your feet? What do your clothes feel like on you? Is there a breeze, if so, what direction is it coming from?
4. With your eyes open, notice the colours. How many different shades of red or blue or orange can you see?

What is the most common colour in your view? What is the least common colour in your view? Now notice the shapes. If you observed your surroundings and had to describe them in terms of shapes only, and not what the objects really are how would you describe them?

5. Finally, appreciate your surroundings.

No matter how noisy or chaotic your present surroundings, when you *really* pay attention and be present you will be surprised at the level of comfort and relaxation you experience. This may simply be the result of knowing your surroundings for what they are instead of making interpretations.

Do this as often as you have time. Especially when you are feeling that your environment might be getting out of control.

Perspective experiment

Try this thought experiment or, provided you take sensible precautions, do it for real. You will need a group of people, a thermometer, and three pails of water: one pail very cold (almost freezing), another at room temperature (around 20°C), a third at about the temperature of the hottest bath you can safely tolerate. Each of you take turns: sit for a *short* time with your left hand in the cold water, at the same time as your right hand is in the 'hot' water, then put both hands into the room temperature water. You will notice that, although both hands are now immersed at the same temperature, the left hand feels that it is in hot water, while the right feels that it is in cold water. Different people will interpret a situation in entirely different ways based on their previous experience.

Your memories, experiences and attitudes build a mental model of the world that act as a filter on incoming information. Your senses – sight, hearing, touch – absorb *everything*. As new information passes through your senses into your brain, you make sense of it by fitting the information into your mental model. This filtering process means that you do not see the *real* world, rather, your interpretation of it.

INSTANT TIP

Chaos is merely a collection of conflicting events and the actions people take to reduce that conflict (no matter how bizarre it might seem to you) always makes sense to them at the time.

03

How do you avoid information overload at work?

Most information overload probably comes from your work environment. Unfortunately, the information that overloads you at work is also frequently the information that carries the greatest consequences if ignored. But not all of it is someone else's fault.

Deal with self-inflicted information overload

We all have our own idea of what 'perfect' means. You could work on something until, in your opinion, it is 'perfect'. Ten people could look at your 'perfect' finished product and each of them might find at least one thing they don't like.

Aiming for perfection only makes sense if, and only if, no one else will have an interest in the outcome. If others are going to have input, then a *compromise* is as good as you will get. For perfectionists, this may be difficult. But if a compromise is not made, the perfectionist will remain overloaded and continue to overload others with trivia.

The two main categories of perfectionist

1. **Time perfectionists**: People who will do *whatever* it takes to meet a deadline. Quality be damned, meet the deadline. This type of perfectionist will find shortcuts to ensure they meet deadlines, often with time to spare. They are so focused on completion that they miss opportunities and different alternatives. They don't take the time to explore options. Working with time-perfect people is also difficult because they are always rushing and creating mini deadlines throughout the project, instead of just letting the project flow. The overload this creates can be catastrophic to a project because the rest of the team won't know what is genuinely urgent and what is urgent only to the time perfectionist.

2. **Quality perfectionists**: People who will sacrifice time for quality. Their motto is, 'if you want it right, you'll have to wait'. The job is not complete until every aspect is checked, double checked and confirmed. The finished product might be perfect, however, as far as others are concerned, packed with flaws (especially if 'being on time' was one of the pre-conditions). This type of perfectionism can be a screen for lack of confidence. If you can't submit work because it's 'not finished/perfect', is it a lack of confidence, fear of disapproval, fear of failure or fear of success that stops you? Those who suffer from quality perfectionism don't believe that anyone can do the job as well as they can, and as a result do more work than would otherwise be necessary.

One of the greatest flaws of a perfectionist is that they don't believe that there is anything wrong with the way they work because they are ... perfect. So, if you recognise yourself in one of these categories, and admit that perhaps the way you work is not 'perfect', then all is not lost.

Solutions

If you are time perfect

The balance that a time-perfect person needs to achieve is the one between quality and time. A time-perfect person needs to develop a sense of realism. They tend to give themselves heroic deadlines, without thinking about what actually has to be achieved. They then get fixated on the time instead of the outcome of the product and they overload themselves from the outset.

The following are some ideas on how you begin to achieve the balance between time and quality.

- When someone asks you how long it will take, pause, take a deep breath, think about what you would normally say, and then double or treble it. If you finish early, then great, but *be realistic*. Give yourself the time to think about quality as well.
- Learn to feel comfortable about extended deadlines. Some deadlines are flexible. There may be time to play with. Do this only once. If you do it too often you may lose credibility. Before you extend a deadline consider what happens to your work when you pass it on. If you extend the delivery date very far beyond the agreed date, it might cause difficulty and inconvenience for those who have to have input to your output.
- If you work in a team on a project and time is a critical factor, it is important to be very clear and honest with

them about the deadlines and what needs to be achieved. Non-time-perfect people will be frustrated if they are given untrue deadlines. If there are ten weeks to complete a project and the time-perfect team leader tells the team that there are in fact only eight weeks, the leader is putting the team in a position of completing what would normally take ten weeks in less than eight. This will undoubtedly have an impact on team performance, stress levels and quality of work. Also, if the team discover that they did in fact have ten weeks, they will lose faith in the leader who will find it very difficult to be taken seriously at a later date. Be honest and be realistic. People are quite capable of managing their own time; you don't have to do it for them.

At the start of the project be honest with the team. Tell them exactly how much time they have to complete the project, create a plan highlighting key dates when parts of the project have to be completed. Make sure everyone has input into the plan and is aware of it.

If you are quality perfect

If you know a quality perfectionist, help them to widen their view of the world. It is important that they consider more than their own idea of a project outcome: perfect for one person does not mean perfect for another. Whether performance, writing, product design or construction, *always* have the audience in mind. Whose opinion really counts? Thousands of small, medium and large businesses fail every year because at some time they build their business around what *they* think is right rather than what the customer wants. Think of the end user. Think of the audience.

When balancing the possible and the perfect, it is important to have a good sense of when good is good enough. Things can always be better but improvement can only happen if there is something to improve on. If you don't close a project and put it into the world, you will never find out what your market would like to improve in it. Needs change and what was once 'perfect' becomes either inadequate or unwanted. The perfect buggy whip has no value if there are no buggies or if whipping is illegal. Unless of course you collect buggy whips.

Achieving balance

'Fit for purpose' should be the new motto of recovering perfectionists. Make it perfect to the degree of 'fit for purpose'. This means that your work should:

- perform the job required
- suit the needs of end users and audiences
- be within time, budget and to specification
- be completed with minimum stress and frustration
- be open to continuous improvement: perfectionists are not keen to allow others to suggest improvements – if it's perfect there is no need for improvement, right?

There are times when perfection is not just necessary, it is a top priority, for example getting the maths perfect for a moon landing or the process exactly right in surgery. In most other cases perfectionism can be a hindrance. Striving for perfection first time round prevents you from trying alternative options, or experimenting.

To avoid overloading yourself and others, have the wisdom to decide when to be perfect, good, excellent, or not to care at all! The skill lies in knowing when perfection is the enemy of excellence.

Ten tips on being a balanced perfectionist

1. Relax. Stop being so uptight.
2. Acknowledge that others are capable of doing a good job.
3. Get the facts and establish what is required rather than imposing your arbitrary decision on what is required.
4. Keep the end user in mind.
5. Have confidence in your work.
6. Be open to criticism, adjustments and improvements to your work.
7. Respect the input of others.
8. Have an open mind with respect to new ideas and alternatives.
9. Don't feel obliged to do everything yourself. Avoid re-work just because it's not exactly what you would do. If the results are the same, then let it be.
10. Sometimes good is better than perfect.

Finish-lines – better than 'deadlines'

'Deadline' is a loaded word. It implies disaster if it isn't met, a bit like a 'Drop Dead Date'. The interesting thing about 'deadlines' is that often there are several attached to most large projects: the one stated at the start of the project, the one you impose on yourself, the one others impose on you, the real one and the delayed one. Be flexible and realistic, and if more time becomes available to complete a project, use it.

Time and pressure

Learn to love it. Controlled stress is healthy. Trouble arises when you have too much to do and you are not in control of it. The more you plan, the more control you will have over events, and the less negative stress you are likely to experience. Balance out stress with recovery time. Take a break, finish work on time, and don't let activity obstruct your sleep. If you are tired, even the most simple events can become disasters.

Thinking time and purpose

You can spend days and days 'doing'. But if you look closely at what you are doing, you might be surprised at how trivial most of it is. If you take time to think about what you want to do and how you want to do it, your time will have much more purpose and the events in your life will have much more meaning. Some of the most important and valuable time is the time you take to think and reflect.

What's the big deal about being late?

If you are late you are wasting someone else's time: that is disrespectful. Sometimes, it can't be helped, but let people know! Henry Ford said 'never complain, never explain'. If you are late, the person you are keeping waiting doesn't need to know all the intimate details of why you are late (unless it relates to them) and they most certainly don't need a made-up excuse. Keep it simple, keep it honest and don't make a habit of it. Being late all the time will only help you to develop a reputation for unreliability. Lateness increases stress for all involved. If you cancel all your other New Year resolutions, try to make this one stick: be on time.

Ten tips on time

1. As far as possible, do one thing at a time.
2. Work on completion. Finish what you start before moving onto the next project or task.
3. Allow for some 'slack' for unpredictable eventualities.
4. Rushing wastes time. Relax.
5. Set realistic deadlines and adapt as 'unknowables' happen.
6. Be clear about how much of your time people can have.
7. *Be present* on the task you are doing. Don't let your mind wander.
8. Make a written plan of your events.
9. Let people who need to be aware of your activities know your plans and changes.
10. Plan for thinking time.

Sometimes the best way to ensure an event fits into the time available is to take a break. Speed and action aren't always appropriate: stop and think.

Think like a genius

What if geniuses are just ordinary people who stumble on a knack or way of thinking that enables them to think and learn more effectively and creatively than others?

'Geniuses' like Newton or Archimedes didn't simply sit under trees or in baths until they became enlightened. They used some very powerful and practical tools to create order out of their thoughts and to find answers to problems that few people ever thought existed, let alone considered solving. The tools used by geniuses are as applicable by you as they are by the great thinkers. These techniques will help you:

- clear your head when faced with a challenging problem
- generate more than one workable solution to a given problem
- think creatively
- think *productively* instead of *re*-productively
- develop a clear methodology that will simplify problem solving.

Some factors common to the world's greatest thinkers

- Idea generation is in *pictures* and *images* rather than words. Einstein and da Vinci drew diagrams instead of writing words and sentences.
- Their thinking is *unrestrained*; **nothing** is rejected until it has been fully investigated.
- They treat thoughts as *things*.
- Ideas are explored using *association.*
- They look at ideas from different *perspectives.*
- They are *prolific* and record everything.
- They fuel their imaginations with *knowledge.*
- Their thinking is *focused.*
- They are *passionate* and *determined* about discovery.
- Instead of seeing *mistakes* and *unexpected results* as failures, they *welcome* them as opportunities to learn how not to do it.
- They see *potential* in everything.
- They never give up.

Thinking differently from usual gives insight into problems. The closer you are to a problem the less able you might be to solve it. Giving yourself space to think allows you to be more creative and to uncover solutions more readily.

Few things are more personal and subjective than the way you learn. Great thinkers have the *will* to try something new, and are happy to get it wrong the first time. They have the *belief* that they are capable of thinking originally and creatively, the *desire* to explore their limits and the *energy* to think.

'I'm thinking all the time,' you might say, 'in fact, I'm thinking so much it's difficult to empty my head!' Take a little time to think about what occupies your mind most of the day. Do you think about yesterday's meeting? Today's agenda? Last night's dinner? Tonight's dinner? An argument you had last week? An argument you would like to have today so that you have the opportunity to say what you wanted to say last week? Do you think about what you have done? Do you think about what you wish you would do? Or do you have new and original thoughts?

Original thinking happens when you look at ideas from a number of different perspectives; when you combine concepts in such a way that your thinking allows you look at the world differently. This type of thinking helps you to learn fast and effectively, and to apply that learning in different contexts. It will help you remember what you learn, and recall it when needed. It will help you be more creative, solve complex problems and communicate more effectively.

Natural selection favours thinkers

Darwin's theory of the 'survival of the fittest' implies the ability to *learn* and, more importantly, to *adapt*. To survive in a complex environment, a species, and for that matter individual members of it, either adapts and thrives, or becomes extinct. The characteristics of an organism play an important role in determining whether it survives as a species. Take a mouse for instance: you might think that a mouse with long legs would have a better chance of surviving than one with short legs – long legs mean it can run faster, escape danger and live another day to reproduce. So, why don't we have supersonic, high-speed, long-legged mice? Long legs have disadvantages as well as advantages. A mouse with very strong long legs needs more food to deliver the energy to move fast. The muscle bulk required for strength and speed means that it will be bigger than its shorter legged counterparts, but there are fewer places that it can use to hide from its enemies. Through evolution, the mouse has developed an optimal length and strength of leg to ensure that it can move efficiently while remaining small enough to hide in places predators cannot reach. While some individual mice might develop extraordinarily long legs, the mouse species in general does not, because it would not be good for the survival of the species as a whole.

Now consider humans and genius: why does only a small percentage of the population demonstrate extraordinary genius? What would be the advantages or disadvantages if the population as a whole were to perform to their highest physical, emotional, psychological and intellectual capacity? What would the world be like if everyone used and developed these talents?

Unlike mice, we are at the top of the food chain. In our cities we have no predators – except for a very small number of other humans – from whom we have to run or hide. There is no reason to limit our development. Yet, despite the potential we are all born with, very few people become the best they can be. I suggest that it's because we are not taught how.

If geniuses, as I have already suggested, are ordinary people who have stumbled on a knack or way of thinking that enables them to think and learn more effectively and creatively than others, then could it be that everyone has the ability to be a Mozart, an Einstein or a da Vinci? Most of these people were as baffled as the rest of us as to how they managed to generate such astonishing ideas, discoveries and inventions. Most stumbled on their 'knack' at such a young age that it was, quite simply, the way they thought and behaved.

The rest of this chapter explores some of the tools the great thinkers in history 'stumbled' on. Think about how you might use each of these techniques to enhance your own thinking skills. To shift from surviving to being supersonic.

Tools for generating genius thinking

Mapping

Before exploring these techniques it is worth talking about information mapping. 'Mind mapping' was formalised and labelled by Tony Buzan in the 1970s. Great thinkers have used similar techniques for centuries. Leonardo da Vinci, Albert Einstein and Thomas Edison, like other geniuses, represented their ideas through diagrams and 'maps'.

You might know them as spider-graphs or thinking maps, but whatever you call them, they all have the same features:

- pictures instead of words
- links between related ideas
- the main concepts in the middle, gradually becoming more detailed towards the end of the branches
- single words or ideas per line
- colour.

Some of the benefits of information mapping and spider-graphs include:

- getting an impression of the bigger picture
- not limited to linear thinking, as when you write an idea in words, sentences and paragraphs
- your mind thinks faster in pictures than it does in words
- links between previously unrelated ideas are quickly and more easily made
- easier to mentally represent a picture than linear text.

Taking spider-graphs a step further

Some people who use spider-graphs generate the information, then immediately get practical with it. However, adding two steps in-between generating the content of the spider-graph and using the information makes it an even more creative and useable learning tool:

1. **Do the generative stage as you would normally:** Write down everything that comes into your head – free associate – don't edit anything out just yet. Write down one word or idea per line.
2. **Change perspective:** Link unlinkable ideas together, write the opposite of what you wrote originally, exaggerate the idea (instead of saying X sometimes happens, say that it always happens or vice versa), change the gender, race, age, political or religious bias of people on the map.
3. **Someone else's shoes:** If, for example, you are in a new job, mentally put yourself in your boss's, customer's, bank-manager's or partner's shoes and re-draw the map. What are the differences between the first and the second map? Now, imagine you are the best in the world at whatever is the main activity of the project, and re-draw the map once more. Open your mind. Write down what comes to your awareness even if it seems to make no sense at all.
4. **Finally, formalise your thinking:** Focus on your outcome. Review the maps you drew at each of the above stages. Select and develop those ideas that you know will contribute most to your project.

System thinking

Edison didn't invent *just* a light bulb, he invented an entire system on which a multitude of light bulbs could function. Thinking in terms of a system will allow you to see the *whole* picture with all its interconnected and interacting components. Integrating the entire system will give a deeper insight and accelerate creative thinking.

Applying system thinking – making sense of a system

1. Write down what you perceive the problem to be (e.g. the general performance of your team is not up to standard).
2. Consider the symptoms that lead you to that view (e.g. late arrival, low motivation, agitated behaviour between colleagues, missing deadlines).
3. List each symptom and write down, against each one, *all* its possible causes. Be as unbiased as possible (e.g. possible causes for missing deadlines – working late hours, unclear job descriptions, unclear management decisions, unreasonable timescales, etc.)
4. Now consider each cause; assess the extent to which each contributes to the situation (e.g. Do people work late hours? Are timescales unreasonable? Is communication between staff and management clear?). It is often worthwhile using an external mediator to remove bias.
5. When you have determined some definite causes, work on what can be done to resolve the issue and prevent recurrence.

One reason this technique works is that instead of accusing your team of poor performance and setting the scene for blame and subsequent denial, you are asking questions that give people the opportunity to examine their performance without feeling singled out or threatened. Asking questions might establish that 'poor performance' is due to people feeling obliged to work late most nights, and becoming exhausted. Unlike 'general poor performance', this is clearly defined. There is now an opportunity to take remedial action.

Now go through steps 1–5 above using 'overload' as the problem you wish to solve.

It's important to carry out this exercise with all the people involved. It's also important to make it a safe and open forum so that people feel free to contribute without thinking that one wrong answer will generate a P45.

'Lily pond'

T.S. Elliot used a system where he started with one idea or theme, surrounded the theme with a number of sub themes, and then repeated that with each sub theme. The end result looked to him like a pond covered in lilies. This technique allows you to explore the theme gradually and in great detail without losing ideas or creating confusion.

Applying the 'lily pond'

1. Build a 9 × 9 grid that will give you 81 squares.
2. Because of the odd number you will have a centre square. State the problem simply and clearly in that square.
3. Around the clearly stated problem, write eight possible solutions (A through to H).
4. Now, write each solution in the centre of each 'lily' square surrounding the centre square.
5. Generate ideas around each of these solutions.

Figure 3.1 illustrates the 'lily pond' grid.

A1	A2	A3	B1	B2	B3	C1	C2	C3
A8	Solution A	A4	B8	Solution B	B4	C8	Solution C	C4
A7	A6	A5	B7	B6	B5	C7	C6	C5
H1	H2	H3	Solution A	Solution B	Solution C	D1	D2	D3
H8	Solution H	H4	Solution H	Problem	Solution D	D8	Solution D	D4
H7	H6	H5	Solution G	Solution F	Solution E	D7	D6	D5
G1	G2	G3	F1	F2	F3	E1	E2	E3
G8	Solution G	G4	F8	Solution F	F4	E8	Solution E	E4
G7	G6	G5	F7	F6	F5	E7	E6	E5

Figure 3.1 The 'lily pond' grid

Ten tips on solving problems, creativity and thinking like a genius

1. Be brave. Think beyond what you know.
2. Stick to the facts.
3. The bigger the problem looks, the greater the need to ensure that it is solved by rational *thinking* rather than *emoting*.
4. Communicate with other minds. Talk. Listen. Ask. Listen again. Get perspectives from people around you.
5. Never assume the first answer is the right one.
6. Develop a positive attitude towards problems. The more you deal with them the better you will get.
7. Never procrastinate, but never make decisions in haste. Whenever you identify a problem, deal with it.
8. Remember: your problem is probably not the greatest problem on earth, neither is it likely to be life threatening. Keep things in perspective.
9. Never let others bully you into action or inaction. If it's *your* problem, *you* solve it. Listen to opinions, but keep your own counsel, unless of course, they have a better idea.
10. Sleep on it. If you can't, then don't try. Just get on with fixing it, but don't do nothing in the hopes that something will happen.

Make problems a family business

My (TK) father has a great attitude towards problems. As kids, my two sisters and I went to him with our problems. He would grin, rub his hands together and say, 'Problems, problems, I *love* problems!' Then he would start us working on our *own* solutions. Kids are smart, let them sort out their own issues; supported by love and, if need be, an appropriate amount of help.

This attitude translates well into business. For a while, positive thinking gurus frowned on the word 'problem' and preferred that we all used the more enlightened term 'challenge'. If a 'challenge' is something you want to avoid, you'll avoid it just as easily as you would a 'problem'. Don't get caught up in semantics. Rub your hands together, grin and say: 'I love problems!' That way, you'll look out for them and catch them when they're small instead of when they become a big 'challenge' and a little more difficult to deal with.

Meetings and your time

Meetings can be one of the biggest time-wasters and anyone attending one can almost guarantee they will leave with more work than they went in with.

Saving time at meetings

- Have a clear agenda agreed by all parties up front.
- When writing the agenda, have three categories of topics:
  1. Topics that *have* to be discussed (vital and crucial).
  2. Topics that *should* be discussed (important but not vital).
  3. Any other business. Don't leave A.O.B. to the end of the meeting. It is the end of the day, people may be tired and (should be) wanting to get back to work. If there is too much A.O.B. the quality of discussion is not good. You will physically or mentally lose many of the attendees and there will be no definite time limit because the A.O.B. time is undefined. So, write the

Sticking to the agenda

A while back I (*TK*) did quite a bit of work for one of the largest organisations in the world. One of my tasks was facilitating meetings. Often I attended a meeting about which I was briefed only half an hour before. In effect, I knew nothing about the content of the meeting (I was not a professional in the technical side of their business) but I did get to know the personalities of the people who attended. My job was to make sure that everything that was on the official agenda was discussed, dealt with and concluded. These meetings would sometimes last a full day. My biggest challenge was those people who decided that the meeting was a good way of getting out of work for a day. They would arrive, drink copious cups of coffee, catch up with their friends, write up their own agenda and then make it their aim to disregard the official agenda in order to fit in their own idea of what should be covered.

The fact that I was not a professional in the subject matter was important, because I had no vested interest in what was being said (that was the job of the chair). I was only concerned with the *time* and *events*. As soon as someone's personal agenda started up I had great delight in diplomatically, but sometimes very firmly, moving on with the formal agenda. Because I wasn't a part of the company and thus not tied up in the internal politics, no one objected when I broke their personal agendas. If they tried to object I would ask them what relevance their point had to the agenda at hand. They often had to work hard to convince me, and the rest of the group that it had any relevance at all. From my experience facilitating meetings that lasted anything from a few hours to several days, here are a few tips on how to save time during meetings and leave without being overloaded.

agenda, send it around and tell people to add any other business they want to include, then predetermine the time you will allow for A.O.B. If it is not included before the meeting, it doesn't get discussed.

● Start exactly on time. Don't recap for late comers.

● When you are chairing or facilitating a meeting the most important thing to do is to prevent time-wasters from taking over the agenda and waffling.

● Have someone take very clear and full notes. The person who takes the minutes should have some knowledge of the subject but should not be biased. The person who takes the notes should *not* be expected to contribute to the meeting.

● Set and adhere to times for oxygen breaks.

● Take a break at least every 90 minutes.

● At the start of the meeting, write up the exact agenda and the timing i.e. points 1–4 before the first break, points 5–7 before the second break etc.

● As the meeting progresses, cross off the subjects covered. Don't retrace your steps.

● Always have a facilitator; it is their job to keep the meeting moving. If the meeting is large and long, get someone from outside the company. The facilitator, like the minutes taker, cannot take part in the discussion. The facilitator must be assertive, firm and respected by those attending. Timing is the facilitator's number one responsibility. If the meeting moves in such a way that it becomes clear that more discussion is needed then it is the facilitator's responsibility to make any changes to the agenda to make sure the timing still works. The facilitator cannot be shy or shrinking. He or she must take control of the meeting from the very start.

- The chair is responsible for content although the facilitator can help with this. As soon as delegates begin to waffle or go off subject, the chairperson (with the assistance of the facilitator) must get them back on subject. Waffling is one of the greatest of all time-wasters at meetings. Some people seem to make it their aim to speak rubbish at meetings. Make it clear, with a smile, at the beginning of the meeting that this will not be tolerated.
- Don't try to fit too much into any meeting.
- Don't run meetings for the sake of it. If you have a scheduled meeting every morning or every Friday, make sure there is a clearly understood, specific reason for it. Don't make meetings a habit.
- Full-day meetings are *never* as effective as those that last only a few hours. Keep them short and to the point.
- Don't invite known time-wasters to meetings unless you can contain them or use their talents.
- Don't make meetings open to anyone who wants to come unless necessary.
- Stop at the end of the meeting. The temptation is to carry it on in the halls outside the meeting. Once it's done, it's done.
- Make action come out of your meetings. Everyone must be clear about *what* exactly is to be done, *who* is to do it, *who* will follow up and *when* the follow-up will happen. People can be quick to agree to do something because it makes them look good; carrying it through is a different matter. The time that will be spent carrying out the actions arising from a meeting is more valuable than the time spent at the meeting.
- Don't waste anyone's time by creating senseless, unlimited or unallocated actions out of meetings.

Meeting checklist

1. Do you have a good reason for arranging the meeting?
2. What specifically is it?
3. Will the meeting disrupt workflow close to a deadline? If yes, is it essential?
4. What is your expected/desired outcome?
5. What personal agendas do you expect from your team (are there any unresolved team issues that might come up during the meeting)?
6. Do you have an agenda?
7. Is it clear, realistic and relevant?
8. Are there 'rogues' on the agenda (issues you have been trying to avoid but shouldn't)?
9. Are the right people coming?
10. Is there an equal mix of easy and difficult people attending (if you only have meetings with people who agree with you, you will never make real decisions)?
11. Are all members fully briefed?
12. Who will take the minutes?
13. Is a facilitator required? If yes, who will do it (depending on facilitation styles, the facilitator and the minutes keeper might be the same person)?
14. Have all actions from the previous meeting been done (don't come to the meeting with excuses)?
15. Have you set a general social gathering with your team? If not, do it.

In brief

- Make meetings part of your work – if they don't accomplish anything, stop them.
- Keep them short.
- Get feedback at the end of each meeting.
- Be honest with your team.

INSTANT TIP

Even if you are lucky enough to be doing your ideal job, work is still only a part of your life. Don't use it as an excuse not to live.

04

How do you avoid information overload at home?

In Chapter 3 we discussed how to avoid information overload at work. For many parents, however, home is the office and children are the clients. Additionally, with or without children, you might feel like every spare moment is spent either paying for bricks and mortar or maintaining them.

Decide what is important: the 'oily beam' test

Imagine you and I are standing at opposite ends of an empty room, approximately ten metres apart. Starting at your end and ending at mine, I draw two parallel lines about half a metre apart. I say to you that if you can walk between the two lines towards me you can have the £10 in my hand. No tricks. All you need do is walk. Would you do it? Probably.

Next, we put two chairs in the room, one at your end of the room and the other at mine. Then get a very strong piece of wood, ten metres long and half a metre wide. Secure each end on either chair. I stand at one end, you at the other. If you walk along the plank, without falling, you can have the £20 I have in my hand. No risk, no danger.

Now imagine you are out of the room. Think of two very tall buildings in a city that you know. We are on top of them, standing at least 50 storeys high. You are on one and I am on the other. A steel 'I' or 'H' beam, about half a metre wide, is placed between the buildings and is securely bolted at each end. I invite you to walk along the beam. You have to walk upright, and you have to stay on the beam. If you were to fall off you would very probably die. Would you do it for £50? Would you do it for £500 or £5,000? How much would I have to offer before you will cross that beam? A million? Ten million? Not at all?

We now know how much money would get you to walk along the beam. Let's complicate it now. It has suddenly become dark. The wind is gusting. It is beginning to rain. There is a fine film of oil on the beam. Now, you have to cross the oily, wet beam in windy conditions, remaining upright. Would you do it? For £50, £5,000, £5,000,000, £20,000,000? Or would all the money in the world not tempt you?

Now, take a moment to think about the *really* important things in your life: family, friends, careers, homes, possessions, dreams, things that are important to you.

So you are on the top of the building, I am on the other. The wet, oily beam is between us. The wind is blowing. I have a large bag in each of my hands. The two things you value most highly are in those bags. You have 30 seconds to cross the beam or one is taken away from you forever. I get to choose which one. Would you cross?

Go through your list. Imagine that I am holding your family in one hand and your friends in the other, which would you choose? Imagine I have your career in one hand and your family in the other, which would you choose? Imagine I have your career in one hand and your dreams in another, which would you choose? Imagine I have your dream job in one hand and your home in another, which would you choose? As you go through your list you will be able to organise your values in a way that shows you what is most or least important in your life. When you build your future, consider your values. Remind yourself of what is important to you. Stick to those and you cannot go far wrong.

Decide what's important – prioritise your time and decide what information you need to support life rather than mould your life around the information that bombards you.

Achieve balance

If it seems to you that you don't have time for anything and are stressed as a result, it will certainly be worth your while to review how you spend your time and determine whether the actual things that you do each day are consistent with your values. Sometimes, you can be pulled into doing what you think you should do instead of what you want to do (for example, allowing work to totally take over your life!). The key thing to remember is that you have choice. The closer your activities are to your core values, the more rewarding the result will be.

Which sounds better to you: choosing how much time you are going to allocate to each event or choosing what events you want to fill your time? Or is it a mix of both?

You have no choice about how much time you have. You do have a choice about how many events you fit into the time you have. The following activity will help you identify which of your typical activities correspond to your values and will help you decide if you are spending your time well.

1. Make a pie chart like that in Figure 4.1. Divide it into sections that show how you spend your available time (waking hours) during a typical week. If you want to, subdivide the work section with the categories of your work activities.

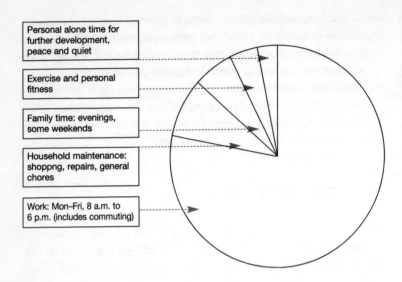

Personal alone time for further development, peace and quiet

Exercise and personal fitness

Family time: evenings, some weekends

Household maintenance: shoppng, repairs, general chores

Work: Mon–Fri, 8 a.m. to 6 p.m. (includes commuting)

Figure 4.1 Example of a time management pie chart.

2. Now, build your own. This chart should represent how you presently spend your time during a typical week.

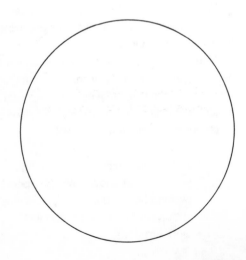

3. Once you have completed your pie, return to the 'oily beam test' outlined above and place each activity or category of activities on the beam to determine what is really important to you and nearest your values.

4. Once you have done that, divide the next circle according to your values and compare the two circles i.e. how much time you spend focused on what's important to you versus the time you spend on activities that are of little value to you.

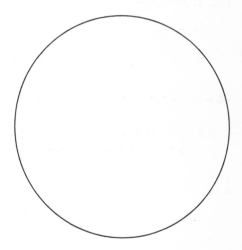

Although it may not always seem like it, you do have a choice. You can always say 'no', you can say 'yes', you can say 'maybe'.

Fitting life and dreams together

One of the most important things about time management is reality. When you dream and plan you can be as boundless as you like. When you act on your dreams you need to be realistic. Your actions take place in the real world. It is important to know that you can achieve a great deal in a short amount of time if you manage your events carefully.

Planning and preparation is the key to managing life and information overload. Whether organising your day or an entire project, the same principles apply:

1. Decide what you want to do.
2. Determine how much time you want to give to each act, task or vision.
3. Plan as much detail as you can, including possible contingency plans.
4. Take action – one at a time, completing tasks as you go.

Planning strategy for fitting it all in

If you have a demanding job and a full family life and still have other projects, it will take careful planning to make it happen. I have used the system described below for many years. It works. Most people with full lives use some form of planning system. Many people only take into account their work activities, and wonder why the other aspects of their life seem neglected. This system accounts for *all* your time and *all* the events you want in your life.

1. Review the 'oily beam' test pie chart allocating your time. Make a list of your different roles and projects, e.g. family, social, job related, hobby, holiday plans, special project, personal development, financial management, etc.

2. Based on the future you want to create, determine the outcome you want to achieve for each item on the above list over a period of four to six weeks (I found four weeks was not quite long enough while six weeks gave me time to do what I wanted).

3. Allocate time for mental and physical holiday times (breaks and breathers).

4. Next to each activity on the six-week list, jot in the approximate time you want to spend on the job and when you are going to do it. Write this in pencil because you will find that things change.

5. Then, in your daily planning system (or whatever system you use), divide your day in half: work related events and non-work related events. In the 'to-do' part of the planner write in all the activities from your six-week list that are due to be done on that day. Make sure that you only put in what you can fit in to the time available.

Evaluation

At the end of each week, month or six-week period, go back to your plans and evaluate how you did. Measure this by reviewing what you did during the period. Where are you giving yourself too much or too little to do? Refer to your pie chart. How are you spending your time? What is not getting done? Does it really matter? Does it reflect your values? Are you getting everything done?

This system will help you ensure that you plan and design how you will achieve your dreams by carrying out concrete, specific action to make them happen. Well managed time, means well managed events within the time available.

INSTANT TIP

Let your family be responsible for their own lives. You don't have to control everything. Back off and give them some space.

05

How do you manage written information?

Occasionally, reading slowly is essential but sometimes, you simply need to get through information, find what you need and clear your in-tray. That is where an effective reading strategy becomes useful.

As well as providing a five-step strategy for managing any written information, this chapter will include techniques on how to:

- organise information for easy access
- remember what you read
- find relevant information quickly
- speed-read without ruining your leisure reading.

The purpose of this chapter is to give you everything you need to:

- **find** information quickly
- make studying **easy**
- **read** non-fiction material **faster**
- **remember** technical and complex material
- **clear** clutter in minutes
- **process** books quickly and easily

- **apply** what you read
- read **smart**
- read with **purpose**.

As the term implies, speed-reading is about reading *fast*. But there is more to it than that. For new information to have any value, you need to *retain*, *integrate* and *apply* it.

Thinking about speed-reading might raise questions such as:

- What is the fastest possible reading speed?
- How do I remember what I read – when I need to remember it?
- How do I maintain concentration when reading technical or scientific material?
- Is speed-reading easy to learn?

If there is a limit on the speed at which people can read, we don't yet know what that limit is. Some people can read a book the size of *War and Peace* in less than twenty minutes and retain and recall enough to answer questions at least as well as those who read 'normally'!

The ability to retain and recall is the most relevant outcome of reading. If you do not intend to remember at least some of what you read, why read it?

The effective reading system described here works by using a five-step process. Follow the guidelines and you will easily and quickly learn to read and manage new information fast and effectively.

Five steps to easy information management

The five-step system is a structured method. It will help you:

- explore the material using at least three different ways
- find information that is relevant to you without missing out what is important
- find the information you require quickly
- integrate new information with what you already know
- accurately recall new information when you need it.

Become familiar with the five-step system. Then adapt it: combine or omit steps to suit your purpose and the style of other non-fiction material (e.g. newspapers, articles, memos, books or magazines).

The five-step effective reading system: organise your reading

If you understand something, it is easier to remember. Imagine reading a book on an unfamiliar subject, or trying to remember material when you don't understand terminology, themes, concepts or jargon. Compare that to remembering new information on a subject you are familiar with.

The purpose of the five-step system is to ensure you:

1. find exactly what you need without having to read irrelevant or unnecessary material
2. never miss relevant information
3. understand, retain and recall information by becoming familiar with structure, content, language and concepts.

For a book of about two hundred pages, Steps 1 to 4 of the system described below could take between five and fifty minutes depending on the depth of information you want. The time for Step 5 will depend on the amount of information you want.

Step 1: Prepare

Preparation should take no more than five minutes.

Lack of focus interferes with concentration and frustrates your reading. By contrast, preparation helps you focus. Your aim is to highlight areas that you want to study and to exclude what you decide is unnecessary.

Establish your purpose and prepare. Ask yourself these questions:

1. What do you *already know* about the subject?
2. What do you *need to know* (is it general information or is it the answer to a specific question)?
3. How and when do you *intend* to use the new information? (Essay, exam or report? General interest? A presentation? When? Next week? Next month? Next year? Or do you need it in ten minutes?)

Step 2: Structure

Take an overview of the material to familiarise yourself with the structure:

- What does it look like?
- How is it organised?
- Are there summaries or conclusions?
- Is the book mainly words?
- Are there pictures?
- What is the print size?

- Is the information organised in sections?
- Is it a series of paragraphs?
- Are there bullet points?

Depending on your purpose, developing an overview of the structure of a two hundred-page book or document should take between one and ten minutes.

During Step 2:

- Read the front and back covers, the inside flaps, the table of contents and the index.
- Scan the bibliography.
- Determine the structure of the book: chapter headings, sub-headings, pictures, graphs, cartoons and images.
- Mark parts of the book that you are sure you will not need.
- Highlight areas you will need.
- Re-affirm your decision: What do you want from the book?

If it does not contain what you need, put the book away. You will save hours of work.

Step 3: Language

You prepared yourself and studied the structure of the book in Steps 1 and 2. Now, familiarise yourself with the *language*. Is there jargon? Is the language complicated? What do the acronyms mean?

It should take five to ten minutes to become familiar with the language of a two hundred-page book.

- Depending on the page size, scan at about a page every two seconds.

- Highlight words linked to your purpose.
- Study the language: Is it technical? Non-technical? User-friendly? Are you familiar with it?
- Do you need to refer to a dictionary?
- Note the meaning of acronyms.

The speed at which you read is determined by your familiarity with the language. Try to recognise recurring themes or concepts during this step. Highlight points that are particularly relevant for your purpose. If necessary, look up key words and concepts before you begin Step 4.

Step 4: Content

Most well-written material outlines the main element of the chapter in the first paragraph. Similarly, the main idea of each paragraph is usually in the first sentence. So read:

- the first paragraph of every section
- the first sentence of every paragraph (if the paragraph is long, read the last sentence)
- summaries or conclusions.

The more thoroughly you highlight, underline, circle, take notes and make spider-graphs of what you read, the easier Step 5 will be.

Step 5: Purposeful selection

By the time you reach Step 5 you will have:

- determined your purpose
- studied the outline and the structure of the material
- read introductions, summaries, and conclusions
- become familiar with language, themes and general contents
- identified sections that contain the information you require.

Now that you are familiar with the book, select *exactly* what you need or want to read.

And now, learn how to read it *fast* …

Read more words, faster

Most people read at about 150 to 300 words per minute. And here's why: as you read this paragraph, do you hear your own voice in your head 'saying' the words you read? If you do, then you are *reading to yourself*. This happens because of how you were taught to read. It is the reason why you read at the same speed that you speak. It's that simple.

Before you learned to read, you learned to recognise one letter or sound at a time. When you mastered that, you progressed to recognising one word at a time. You read out loud. That enabled your teacher to check that you recognised and pronounced the words accurately.

Then, instead of reading out loud to yourself, you read silently. You spoke to yourself. That led to a belief that you have to hear every word to comprehend what you read. You don't! Your 'inner voice' became a habit. That's what we're about to change.

You could say that you learned to read with your ears instead of your eyes.

At first you were still learning to recognise the words. 'Reading to yourself' was slow. As your vocabulary increased, you recognised words more quickly. Your reading rate increased until it stabilised at the same words per minute at which you speak. **But your reading *strategy* did not change.**

The aim is to help you change that strategy: to change the old belief that you have to read with your ears.

Read with your eyes

To increase your words-per-minute reading rate you must accelerate your reading speed until you transform the old habit of sounding out the words in your head (often referred to as sub-vocalisation).

Two methods for achieving this are:

1. The guide

- Place a guide (pen, pencil, or finger) underneath the first or second word of a line.
- Move the guide smoothly across the page from the beginning of a line to the end of that line.
- Repeat on each line.
- Move the guide a little faster than is comfortable.
- The movement needs to be smooth and swift.

If you pause the guide, you are *following* your eye instead of *leading* it. If you sub-vocalise, your speed will not increase. When the guide moves quickly and smoothly, your eyes are forced to follow. Your reading rate will increase. The faster you move the guide, the less you will sub-vocalise. Your inner voice will be unable to keep up. The aim is to eliminate the habit of reading one word at a time and to stop your attention wandering.

Speed-reading is a skill. It is easy to learn. Developing that skill does not mean you have to read fast all the time. Technical content, print size, mood, familiarity with the subject material and your purpose can affect reading speed. The ability to read quickly allows you to choose how fast or slow you want to read.

2. Selective reading

When you read material on a familiar subject and you don't want to miss out important items in the text, use this technique.

- Read the first sentence of the paragraph.
- Skim the rest of the paragraph for key words, and, only if you think it's necessary.
- Read the last sentence of the paragraph.

Concentration is focused attention

If you read without paying attention, you will not remember what you read.

Attention:

- Is **dynamic**. Focus on one thing only. Notice how long it takes for your mind to wander.
- Has to be **undivided.** Try listening to more than one conversation at a time. You will hear bits of each but you are unlikely to absorb either fully.
- Follows **interest**. Boredom extinguishes attention.
- Is maintained by a series of **discoveries,** new ideas and insights.

There are several categories of attention:

Voluntary: When you voluntarily pay attention to something you do so naturally. When you are totally absorbed in what you are doing and distracted by nothing you don't have to force yourself to concentrate.

Involuntary: When you carry out routine tasks, for example, when driving you arrive at your destination and can't immediately recall the journey.

Dispersed: Too many simultaneous activities or lack of interest can cause a sense that 'everything attracts your attention at once'.

Aim to improve your ability to focus your attention voluntarily and to focus attention fully even in situations where it once was difficult to concentrate.

The more interested you are in what you are doing, the easier it is to concentrate. Can you remember when you were last so engrossed that you lost awareness of time? Nothing distracted your attention. You were interested and motivated towards a goal.

Concentration increases when you have:

1. **Goals** – you know what you want.
2. **Motivation** – you know why you want it.
3. **Interest** – you want it!

If reading material is boring, or if it is hard to find motivation or interest, take deliberate action:

- Close your eyes.
- Breathe deeply and take a little time to become still.
- Gather your thoughts and ask yourself what your purpose is.
- Write down your reasons for reading the material.
- How long do you estimate it will take?
- What is challenging about the text? What is easy?
- How will you apply what you learn?
- How will you benefit?

If your mind drifts, focus your attention by speaking *out loud* as you write down your plan and your concentration will improve. Your desire to complete the task will take over.

Remember what you read

No matter how fast you read, unless you intend to remember what you read you will have wasted your time. Without concentration, retention and recall is almost impossible.

If you can daydream, you can concentrate

Do you ever daydream? Gaze through the classroom window ... contemplate the wall as your computer screen flickers at the edge of your awareness ... drift somewhere pleasant as someone talks to you? Your eyes glaze ... stare into space ... absorbed in your thoughts.

When you daydream, you focus. You concentrate. You are absorbed to the exclusion of everything else.

The top three methods for remembering what you read are:

1. **Use new information:** Explain. Discuss. Write. Construct arguments for and against. Think. Apply.
2. **Have a purpose:** Always have a reason for reading something.
3. **Think ahead:** Think about *when* you intend to use it. The method you use to remember new information will vary depending on *why* and *when* you will use the new information. If you are reading complex information, the method you use to understand, retain and apply it will differ from the method you would use if you only need a general understanding of that material.

Other memory techniques

Linear

Make notes as you read or after each section. Include your thoughts, ideas and cross-references. The more you include your own ideas, the more reliable your long-term memory is likely to be.

Key words

Highlight words that carry the message. If you make separate notes, avoid making a list of key words that makes no sense when you review it later.

Margin reading

A book communicates ideas. Take ownership. Add your thoughts to the author's. <u>Underline</u>, (circle) , and highlight essential areas. Decide whether you agree or disagree. Note your reasoning. Highlight what you do understand. <u>Underline</u> what you don't understand then highlight it when you understand it.

Naturally, do this *only* with books that belong to you, or use sticky notes.

The aim is to 'interact' with the text.

Spider-graphs

- Place the primary idea (body) in the centre of a horizontal page.
- Secondary ideas form thick branches (arms and legs) from the centre.
- Tertiary ideas (fingers and toes) flow from secondary ideas. And so on until you reach the finest detail.
- Use colour and symbols.
- One word or idea per line.

Improve speed and memory

These exercises help improve memory and increase speed.

Stretch your memory

Read one page as fast as you can, using a guide. Stop. Summarise what you remember. Read five to ten pages like this every day. Gradually increase the number of pages. Start with a familiar subject. Attempt more challenging material as your ability and confidence increases.

Stretch your speed

The 'one minute trip'

- Read for one minute. Count how many lines you have read.
- Read for another minute. This time read two lines more.
- Then read four lines more. Then six more. Then eight more. Then ten more and so on.

As you practise and your concentration improves, stretch the 'one minute trip' to two minutes, then four, then six, then eight minutes … and so on.

Always read for good comprehension and recall. As soon as you sense that you are unlikely to remember what you read, stay at that speed until you feel comfortable that you can gradually increase speed.

Reading quickly requires concentration. If you don't understand what you read, you will not remember it easily. When this happens, your concentration will fade and you will most likely become bored and disappointed.

Metronome pacing

Invest in an electronic metronome from a music store.

- Set the metronome at a slow speed.
- Read one line per 'tick'.
- Every half page or so, increase the pace of the metronome by one beat per minute until you reach the fastest speed.
- Do this for two minutes.
- Relax for five minutes.

The metronome will reach a speed at which you will not be able to read every word. This 'pushes' your eye and your brain to absorb more than one word at a time *without* sub-vocalisation. This gradually stretches your ability. When you sense that you cannot take in what you read, maintain that speed. Make sure that even though you may not take in the content, you see and recognise (but not say) every word.

All reading material is not equal

You've looked at the five-step reading system, speed-reading and some memory strategies. Now it's time to look at what you read and how to apply the different techniques to ensuring you get most out of them.

Reading different types of material

The way you approach a document (book, newspaper or memo) should be driven by your purpose: Why are you reading it? When will you use the information next?

Technical material

This type of reading can be fairly easy because most technical writing is well structured. Also, you rarely have to read and remember everything about the text without being able to refer to it later on when you need it. Apply the five-step system in its entirety for this type of reading and use a memory technique that works well for you. Try spider-graphs and if you don't like spider-graphs, try a process map. These techniques allow you to see how information, ideas and practices are linked and what effect they have on each other.

Non-fiction for leisure

This is perhaps the easiest of all reading simply because you are already relaxed and interested in the subject (the ideal positive learning state). Most non-fiction, like technical writing, is also fairly well structured so the five-step process can be readily applied.

It is easy to become absorbed in 'work' related reading and not put time aside for leisure reading and knowledge gathering. Once you are comfortable with speed-reading and the five-step system you may find that this is the ideal type of material to practise on. Enjoy taking the time for this type of reading. If you have much work to do you might feel uncomfortable or guilty about taking time out for leisure reading albeit non-fiction. A good way to get around this is to make part of your purpose increasing your reading skill so that you will be able to read work material more effectively. If you only ever read texts that bore you, your passion for reading will soon be subdued. Make time to read what you want to read.

Reading for research

The good thing about reading for research is that your purpose is normally very clearly defined and you are looking for something quite specific. Apply the five-step system and follow the guidelines for 'reading for study'. If you are studying and working at the same time, Chapter 9 will give you ways of organising all your reading from the start of the course to the end of the exam.

Reading for work (especially mail and memos)

The rule here is 'be selective'. The trouble with the reading you do for work is that there can be an activity attached to every document. Before you read anything, especially if it is long and you think it might take you a while or, if it seems to land on your desk often, ask a few questions first:

- Who wants you to read it?
- Why do they want you to read it?
- What are you likely to have to do with the information as a result of reading it?

Once you have established that there are good reasons for reading the documents, take the following steps:

1. **Decide** how much time you will devote to reading incoming mail or memos.
2. **Preview** the documents with one thing in mind – can this go in the bin? Then sort them into two piles, one of which goes straight into the bin, the other requires further attention.
3. **Passive read or skim** all of the documents in the remaining pile and ask one question of each – can this be filed or does it require action? Put aside the pile for filing.
4. **Actively read** the remaining pile, and, using sticky notes or writing directly onto the letter or document, note the actions that need to be taken.
5. Finally, **plan** the actions into your day or week, then file the documents into the appropriate file so that you can retrieve them easily when you need them.

> **Tip**
>
> Remember the clear desk policy – only have papers on your desk for the job you are currently working on.

Newspapers

Note: This does not apply to the casual relaxed reading of the Sunday morning paper unless you want it to. Reading a newspaper should be approached with the same preparation as any other reading. The five-step system works very well for papers, however, it may not be necessary to use all five steps in order. You can read a paper very quickly by following three very simple steps:

1. **State your purpose:** are you reading to gain an overview of the whole paper or are you looking for a particular story?
2. **Preview and passive read** the entire paper by looking at the headlines and reading the first paragraph of any stories that look interesting. Circle the articles you would like to return to.
3. **Actively read** the selected articles for the information you want.

To read newspapers effectively:

- Set a time limit and stick to it.
- Read story continuations (often on other pages) as you come to them. This is a good indication of how much attention you pay to reading a paper. If you come to the second part of a story several pages later but cannot remember the details of the first part, take a break.
- Since most of the facts are normally in the first few paragraphs of a story, start reading each story you select

fairly thoroughly at the beginning and then speed up and skim the rest picking up information as you identify it as relevant.

- Ask yourself;
  - What is the position of the paper with respect to its political slant?
  - Have you read articles by the journalist before? Do you like their style?
  - Is this the best paper to read for your purpose?

Unlike most other forms of writing, the structure of a newspaper story can be broken into parts quite easily. A narrative takes you from the beginning of a story to the end and if parts are missed out some of the meaning goes with it. A newspaper isn't as unified as that. A newspaper story can be read with sections missed out of it, you might lose some detail but the story will remain the same. Very little interpretation can be made of most newspaper stories. They are real events involving real people, and are often given an editorial 'flavour', style or angle by the paper and the writer.

Magazines

Magazines (especially special interest or trade magazines) are slightly different from newspapers. A newspaper is one of many sources of news. If you miss anything from the paper, you could get the story from the television, radio or Internet. Most magazines only come out once a month or once a quarter. A magazine should thus be treated like a small textbook. Follow all the steps of the five-step reading system to get the best out of a magazine. If there is information you are likely to need again in the magazine there are several things you can do to make it easily accessible:

- Read the magazine with an adhesive sticky notepad to hand. As you find articles you are interested in note the page number, title and brief summary (just a sentence or two) on the sticky note. Stick the note on the front of the magazine and file the magazine in a file dedicated to 'interesting articles'.

● If you don't want to keep the whole magazine then tear out the pages or photocopy the articles you want and file those away with a brief summary of what the article is about.

● Another very useful piece of information you could put on the sticky note is *why* you thought the article might be useful later on. When you return to it at a later date you will find it easier to place each article in priority. It will also help you when going through the file to see what you no longer require and can throw away.

● Be picky. Most magazine reading is for interest and you are unlikely to be tested on it but you might want to talk about it. So select the articles that interest you and as you read think of how what you read fits into your knowledge bank already.

Novels

The more you read the faster you will become. Reading novels is excellent practice for speed-reading skills. Your reading rate will automatically increase when you are aware of your reading strategy and practise the reading system on non-fiction. With speed-reading skills you will have the choice to read a novel as slowly or as quickly as you like.

If you enjoy novels and you want to read more of them then you may find this strategy useful:

● Preview the book thoroughly (excluding the actual story). Look at the front and back covers, read any author's notes, biography or forward, take a good look at the author's photograph if there is one. Do you like the author's style? Do you like the look of the author? Does the back page blurb intrigue you? What you do at this point will shape your attitude towards the book. Your attitude will determine whether you are likely to enjoy the book or not.

- Next, read the first page. Does it grab your attention?
- If it does and the book passed your preview test then read on and enjoy. If not, then skim the book picking up key words and reading the first few sentences of each chapter. If the book still doesn't catch your imagination then you can choose not to read it.
- If you do decide to read the novel but you don't have much time, then practise 'on-line selective reading' (described below). This technique is for novels or very short pieces of text that don't require the full five-step treatment.
- If you get bored with the story halfway through the book, give yourself permission to put it down. It is the job of the storyteller to keep you intrigued.

Tip

As you read a novel, look only for the pieces of text that carry the story. Skim over the description. Most novels carry the story in conversation between the characters. As you read you will become familiar with the layout and be able to identify where the descriptive text starts and ends. If you begin to really enjoy the novel and want to read everything, then you can choose whether you want to slow down a bit to enjoy the scenery.

E-mails

A blessing or a curse depending on who sends them. Rule one with e-mails is to do to others as you want them to do to you. If you don't want huge letters and memos and masses of junk mail – don't send any unless absolutely necessary! If someone repeatedly sends you e-mails you don't want, whether it's jokes or stories, be firm and straightforward and ask them not to. Like traditional mail, if you can see it is junk before you open the envelope – bin it.

A good way to screen your e-mails is to use the feature that allows you to have your inbox screen split. The top half has a list of all the messages, and the bottom half lets you read the e-mail without actually opening it. This saves time. Some systems have a preview function which allows you to view only the first few words.

If there are attachments to the e-mail and you need to read them fast, it might be better to print them out. If you prefer to read from the screen there are some ideas later in this chapter on how to do this without straining your eyes.

Instructions

Believe it or not, some people have asked me how to read instructions so that they get to finish what they started. Planning is the key. Unlike most other reading, almost every word counts in instructions. Missing one or two could mean you never get to build what you set out to build. Also, most manufacturers write instructions in such a way that they are quick and easy to follow (not necessarily to understand).

Here are some tips on reading instructions:

1. Read through all the instructions before you do anything. Go from step one to the end; don't miss anything out at all. If it looks like a lot or that there is a lot involved in the activity, relax and gather all the information you need first.

2. The first time you read the instructions, mark off phases of the job, breaking the task into manageable chunks that correspond with how you want to manage your time when you do the job.

3. If there are any pictures, study them thoroughly.

4. Once you have read the instructions and have an idea of what the job entails, make sure you have everything you need.

5. After you have gathered everything you need to do the job (tools, equipment, assistant), go through the instructions again, this time focusing on each of the phases you identified in the first step.

6. Do things one at a time. But, while you are following one step, keep the next one in mind so that you know where you are heading.

7. Tick off the steps as you finish them.

8. If you come to a step you don't understand, think of something you did in the past that is similar to the job you are doing now, look at the picture and carry on unless you feel that carrying on will prove to be a disaster. If so, contact the manufacturer or call someone to come and help.

9. Reward yourself once you have finished.

Following instructions is much like following a set of directions. When you can visualise the finished product or the destination then completing the task will be much easier. Remember that many instructions are written in foreign countries and the language might not be accurate.

> **Tip**
>
> If you find some paragraphs confusing, mark them and carry on. If the meaning doesn't become clear as you read, go back to those sections and read them more carefully and perhaps check other sources.
>
> If, however, you become more confused as you read the text, then you may have missed the key word or idea in the whole passage. If this happens:
>
> ● Stop.
> ● Take a short break.
> ● Reassess your purpose.
> ● Follow the first four steps of the five-step system thoroughly.
>
> Selective reading can be very slow and very frustrating if you miss the point of the text.

Critical reading

One of the purposes of reading critically is to evaluate the text. The aim though is to evaluate the *whole* text or argument, finding out the author's intent and judge at the end whether he/she was successful. Here are a few guidelines for critical reading:

- Read with an open mind.
- Know your own opinion before you begin so that you are not unduly swayed by the author's argument.
- Don't jump to conclusions.
- Keep asking questions.

Reading critically and effectively with an open mind

1. Understand the literal meaning of the text. Be sure you understand how the names, dates, figures and facts all fit together.
2. After that, look for the suggested meaning of words and phrases (connotations).
3. Recognise the tone: is the author being sarcastic, honest, factual or whimsical?
4. Create an image in your mind of what the text is about and look for any gaps in the story.
5. Look for any comparisons, metaphors, similes, clichés or other figures of speech.
6. Once you have all the information you need, make a value judgement. Did the author succeed in what he/she set out to do? Are you convinced? If you are not, are you at least satisfied that although you don't agree with the author, the structure is sound? What would it take to convince you? If the author failed, why?

Evaluating non-fiction

To **evaluate non-fiction**, follow the above steps one to six and ask yourself additional questions:

- What assumptions are being made by the author?
- What evidence does the author present?
- Is it true?
- Do the arguments for cause and effect relate to each other?
- Is the conclusion logical?

- Does the author write more on opinion than on research?
- Is the writing emotive?
- What conclusions can you draw?

Evaluating fiction

The difference between evaluating non-fiction and fiction is that an evaluation of a fictional text is based mostly on how you feel about the text, not on fact or what you *know* about a subject: fiction by its nature, while it may contain factual information is full of assumptions and lacking in evidence.

Some questions to ask as you read fiction:

- Is the story believable? Even if it is far-fetched and imaginative, can you believe it?
- Are the characters and events believable? Do they have a purpose or do they seem to exist with no purpose other than get in the way of the story?
- Are conflicts justified or has the story succumbed to violence for its own sake.
- Are the characters superficial? Do you get to know them? Has the author developed them well?
- Does the story lead you or do you find yourself wondering where it is going?
- Does the plot flow?
- Are you gripped and intrigued?
- Do you find it easy to put down or not?

Reading critically will give you the insight into the true value of the text and if you find none, save yourself time and put it down.

In brief

● Everything you read should be approached differently. When you begin, ask yourself: Why am I reading this? When am I likely to need it again? Do I want to remember everything I read? Is this just for reference?

● If you enjoy reading novels, make time to read as many as you can. They are excellent for improving your visual reading skills and for increasing your reading speed.

● Be critical but open-minded when you read. Consider that both you and the author might be wrong.

Your eyes and other vitals

The eyes need rest and relaxation as much as they need exercise. Reading is easier and more enjoyable when the eyes are relaxed.

Prevent eye strain

The muscles that control the eye are small. They need to be exercised carefully. The following will help you exercise the eyes as well as relax them.

1. **Palm:** Rub your hands together for a few moments. When the hands are warm, close your eyes and cover them with your hands. Make sure no light gets in.
2. **Blink:** If you do not blink, your eyes will become dry. Blink often to lubricate them. Put a little note or a sign below your screen to remind you to blink while reading from a PC monitor.

3. **Workout:** Look straight ahead, then look up as far as you can, then down as far as you can, then to the left, then to the right. Then, look to the top-left corner of your visual field, the top right, the bottom right and the bottom left. Hold each gaze for only a couple of seconds. Relax. Gently squeeze your eyes shut then repeat the exercise. After you finish, palm for two minutes.

To help you read from a PC monitor without straining your eyes:

- **Change the font size and type to suit you:** For many people, serif fonts are easier and quicker to read on paper. Most websites, however, are changing to small sans serif fonts. Decide which you prefer.
- **Speed:** When reading from a monitor, try using the 'down arrow' instead of 'page down'. Fix your eyes on the last/second last line of the text and move the text up the monitor a line at a time using the bottom of the screen as your guide. If the document is long, it may be quicker to read if you print it out. Experiment to find which you prefer.
- **Light:** Daylight is best. In artificial light, there should not be too much contrast between the light under which you work and the rest of the room. The main source of light should come over the shoulder opposite your writing hand.

Distractions and solutions

In an ideal world we would read only what interests us, only in the right environment, only when we had as much time as we needed, and only when we wanted to. Life, however, is not like that. We often must read material we are not particularly interested in, at a time and place not suited to our reading style and, all too often, with a deadline.

Distractions are not just what happens around you. Your internal state can be as distracting as a constantly ringing telephone. Distractions hamper effective reading and accurate recall. The more you can reduce them, the more chance you will have of successfully reading what you need in the time you have available.

Concentration

1. Know your purpose.
2. Use a guide, especially if you are tired or if the material is challenging.
3. Make notes as you read.
4. To help maintain concentration, take a break every thirty minutes for approximately five minutes.

If your attention drifts easily, seemingly inconsequential things distract you, and you find it hard to concentrate, an easy solution may exist.

The following will help increase your concentration and your ability to focus on one task.

● To ensure peak concentration, **take breaks often** – approximately five minutes every thirty minutes if you are only reading. If you are reading a number of different texts and taking notes you could stretch your reading time to between forty-five minutes and one hour before you take a five- or ten-minute break. Pay attention to your body as you read. When you start yawning, making mistakes, re-reading passages or if you develop a headache, it is time for a break. If you work through the symptoms of tiredness your concentration, ability to remember and understand what you are reading will diminish rapidly. Taking a break does not mean lying down and going to sleep for twenty minutes (although that does help) – go for a walk, drink some water, do something different.

- Know your **reasons for reading**. The clearer your purpose, the easier it will be to concentrate even if you do not really want to. If you have no reason, however, you will probably give up fairly quickly.

- **Read actively** using a pacer, especially if you are feeling tired or if the material is challenging. The more senses you use, the more alert you are likely to remain. Imagine eating a meal with only the sense of sight. You couldn't smell it, taste it, feel the texture of the food or hear the sounds of cutting and slicing a juicy dish. All you could do was see it and eat it. How much do you think you would enjoy that meal? Most of the enjoyment is in the sensory appreciation of the meal: the taste, smell, texture and presentation of the food. The same applies to reading. Unfortunately we are taught at a very early age to appreciate reading only through *one* sense. When you start building spider-graphs, taking notes, thinking, discussing and actively reading you will find that reading becomes more like the meal you can see, taste, smell, hear and feel. You almost always remember a good meal when the company is good and the surroundings pleasant. Treat reading like a good meal – you'll be surprised.

- Set a definite **time limit**. Break your reading into chunks. The chunks should be small enough to feel easily managed and big enough to feel that you are achieving your goal. Be realistic. If, as you read, you find that the size of chunks are too big or too small, stop and reassess. Be flexible.

- The better your **vocabulary**, the faster your reading. To improve comprehension, underline unfamiliar words during Step 3 of the five-step effective reading system (language). Look up the words at the end of the paragraph, page, and section as appropriate.

Coping with external noise

If you are not one of these people who can concentrate either because of, or in spite of, background noise, do everything you can to minimise the noise around you. Unfortunately, there is always likely to be some external noise you don't have much control over. If you work in an open-plan office you might find the noise in the office distracting. There are several things you can do to minimise distraction from this kind of noise.

- **Earplugs** – if you get the right type they can be very comfortable and effective. Most good chemists will supply them. Try out a few makes, then keep several sets in your desk.
- Wear earphones with **appropriate music**. Music without words and not too loud. Baroque music is best for maximum concentration – approximately 55–60 beats per minute. Make sure it's not too melancholy and only play music you enjoy. Mozart, Vivaldi and some of Beethoven's works are also good for concentration. Experiment with music. Put one composer on for twenty minutes, change to another and then compare how you feel or how well you concentrated.
- If your desk is in a truly **open-plan space** – with no dividers between the desks – creating a visual barrier between you and the rest of the space will help cut distraction. You do not have to build a wall around you, this is not always desirable or possible. All you need do is place something on your desk that reaches eye level. This will provide a psychological barrier between you and the distracting environment and make it easier to cope with.
- If at all possible, leave the noisy environment and find a quiet space to read in.

Getting away from it all

A delegate in one of my (TK) workshops would go into the cleaning closet when he had a very important document to read that needed all of his attention. He would go into the closet, jam the door shut, read the document, take the notes he needed and appear when he was finished. It worked for him and he was lucky enough to have a cleaning closet nearby with plenty of light, a bit of space, a supply of fresh air and no fumes.

Coping with internal noise

Internal noise is caused by your mind wandering, perhaps because you have not decided to spend the time on a particular task. The guidelines on concentration will help you here. What will help most however, is the *decision* to take the time and read.

If you don't make a firm decision to sit down and read, the type of internal talk that goes through your head might sound like this: 'I don't have the time for this ... X really needs to be done now ... Y will have to move to this afternoon ... I should be doing Z ...' There will be so much 'noise' in your head that you will be unlikely to remember one word you have read and will be wasting time.

● Make a decision to allocate a certain amount of time to read a set amount of material. If you can plan it into your day, do so. Some reading cannot be planned for. In this instance, instead of diving into the text without thinking, take time, go through the preparation and preview stages quickly. Then, if you think that the document really does need to be read, decide when you are going to do it and when you will put the time aside.

● After the decision is made, most internal talk will
   disappear and you will be able to focus.

Physical distractions

Tiredness

When you are tired it will be almost impossible to concentrate. If
you can, take a break and go for a short nap or a walk in the park.
If you are unable to do that, there are a several other strategies
open to you:

● Cut the time you spend reading down to ten- to fifteen-
   minute chunks.
● Use multi-sensory reading.
● Drink plenty of water.
● Do aerobic exercises during your breaks – jump up and
   down a bit to get the oxygen flowing.
● Breathe deeply and stretch every few minutes.
● If you have music playing, make it upbeat and energetic.
● Make sure you have a *very good reason* for reading
   through your tiredness.
● Do not go on more than you have to – stop when you are
   finished and take a good rest.
● Avoid working through the night.
● Avoid sugar or starch.
● Avoid caffeine. For maximum performance you want to be
   alert not jittery.
● Reading at the right time of day can go a long way to
   preventing tiredness. You may notice that you can
   concentrate better at certain times of day. Your results will
   be better if you read at those times.

Sore eyes

Any kind of physical discomfort is a distraction. Your eyes are your primary tool for reading – take care of them.

Stress and reading

If you are stressed it is better to stop for a short time, even if you think you don't have the time. Stop, breathe, relax, evaluate the job, have a cup of tea or water and carry on. Being stressed does not make you read any faster or more effectively.

Hunger and thirst

Hunger is a serious distraction. Similarly, if you eat too much, concentration will be impaired. If you have a large amount of reading to do, avoid eating too much at once and avoid excess sugar and starch. Another cause for poor concentration is dehydration. Your body is 90 per cent water, and by the time you feel thirsty you are already dehydrated. Drink plenty of water even if you don't feel like you need any. Avoid tea and coffee as the caffeine in them will dehydrate you more than a lack of water will.

Environmental issues

Comfort

Ensure you have fresh air and adequate light. Make yourself as comfortable as possible without feeling sleepy.

Light

Daylight is best. If there is none, then there should not be too much contrast between the levels of light under which you are working and the rest of the room. This helps prevent eye strain. The main source of light should come over the shoulder opposite to your writing hand.

Desk and chair

Make sure your desk and chair are the right height. When you sit on the chair you should be able to sit back in the chair supporting your back with your feet flat on the floor. If you cannot reach the floor, place a block at your feet. Your desk should be large enough to take everything you need for the work you are undertaking.

Work distractions

Plan your day

Distractions come easily when you don't know what you want to achieve. At the start of your day write down everything you want to achieve, including the reading you want to do. Set aside time for it. It might also be useful to put time aside in your plan for leisure reading. Once you plan it and you can see that reading a novel for a while isn't going to mean that you will not achieve everything else in your day, you will find that you enjoy the time, still get everything done and improve your speed-reading by reading more.

Set ground-rules

Once you start something, don't let anything distract you from completing it unless there is a very good reason. Have you ever started mowing the lawn or doing the dishes only to get distracted onto something else and then you don't really want to go back to it? Once you start something, *finish it*. This will not only improve the quality of your work, it will increase the quantity of what you can achieve. You will also feel more relaxed and at ease because the job has been done.

People demanding your attention

Few people have the luxury of being able to work without interruptions. There will always be someone, somewhere demanding your attention at some point, whether by phone, in person or e-mail.

If you can, set aside the time you need to read and put up a 'do not disturb' notice.

If you are unable to do that, and most of us are, deal with interruptions like phone calls and people wanting to see you by consciously breaking off from your reading task and paying attention to the interruption.

If the phone rings or someone comes up to you while you are reading:

- If possible, finish the sentence or paragraph you are on.
- Place a mark on the place where you stopped.
- Briefly revise in your mind or on paper your understanding of the last sentence you read.
- Then, give attention to the next task.

Once the interruption is over, you can return to your reading:

- Sit for a moment and recall your understanding of the last sentence you read.
- Re-affirm your intention and purpose for reading.
- Set the time again for a manageable chunk.
- Continue to read.

Habit dictates that when we are interrupted we are very likely to 'hop' from one task to another. Instead of doing this, take a brief pause between tasks to ensure that you don't waste time trying to find where you left off before the distraction, doing this will prevent you from having to sort out your ideas and remove confusion from your mind when you get back to the task.

Clearing your desk of distractions

Mail

If you get a lot of mail at the beginning of the day, have a routine of twenty minutes maximum each day to open all your mail and file it, deal with it or bin it. Don't let anything get in the way of doing that. It might not seem an important job at the time but when a week's mail piles up on your desk undealt with it can be very distracting and waste more time than a short amount of stress-free time spent every day.

Desk space

Every piece of paper on your desk will distract you several times every day. To minimise this type of distraction make sure that the only things on your desk are those that have something to do with the project at hand. If you have your 'in' and 'out' trays on your desk, find another place for them for a week. At the end of the week, assess how differently you spend your time. As long as the tray is on your desk, you only have to look up and you will see everything else you have to do that day instead of being able to focus on *one* job at a time.

Clutter

If your desk tends to be full of paper, clear it of *everything* other than the job at hand – for just one day – and see the difference. At the end of each day, make sure you leave your desk totally clear. In the morning you will feel far more relaxed and able to choose what you want to deal with instead of having to deal with whatever happens to be on the top of the pile.

Other people's reading

Do not let anyone put anything on your desk that you haven't seen and agreed to have there, *especially* if you have to read it. When someone gives you something to read ask them to explain clearly why they think you have to read it, then decide if you want to accept it as an activity in your schedule. If they cannot give you a satisfactory reason, think carefully before you accept it because once you have, you will have to commit the time required to doing it.

In brief

- Take breaks often.
- Make sure you have a reason for reading.
- Read actively.
- Set a definite time limit for your reading.
- Wear earplugs or earphones if the noise around you is distracting.
- If possible, find a quiet space to read if you have something that requires your full attention.
- Be aware of what you eat and drink while you work. Your diet has a great affect on your ability to concentrate.
- Take care of your eyes.
- Plan your day and leave space for unexpected requests on your time.
- Work in a clear space. Have only the paperwork relating to the job at hand on your desk.
- Avoid accepting reading material from people until you are sure you have to read it.
- Spend a maximum of twenty minutes a day sorting through your mail and e-mails.

Points to remember

1. Have a clear, definite purpose.
2. Use a guide.
3. Split the reading task into thirty-minute chunks.
4. Read actively; take notes, write in margins, circle, highlight, underline and create spider-graphs.
5. Use the new information: discuss, teach, write reports, etc.
6. Refer to notes from books you have read previously.
7. Enjoy the process.
8. Ensure you are comfortable and that you have adequate light.
9. If you *must* read a book rather than *want* to, divide the task into thirty-minute chunks. Then read for *only* thirty minutes at a time. Take a break for five minutes. Reflect on your purpose: what will you get if you read it? What will you get if you don't?
10. Cross-reference ideas. Think of possible links between sources.
11. Focus and concentration will ensure you read faster, comprehend what you read and recall the new information easily.
12. Remember: you don't have to read fast *all* the time. Be flexible.
13. When you encounter a word you don't understand, wait until the end of the page or chapter to look it up unless it stops you understanding the whole piece.
14. If you use the five-step strategy for novels you'll spoil the ending! When reading novels you can still experiment with different reading speeds.

What next?

The only part of the smart reading strategy that requires a little practice is the speed-reading (reading more words at a time). Take a few minutes each day to read as fast as you can. Use a guide. Push to increase your reading rate each day. After you break the habit of reading with your ears, progress comes quickly.

Focus and concentration will suffer if you view reading as tedious. If you think of it as fun, interesting or valuable, concentration, comprehension and recall will improve. The five-step system 'chunks down' the task so that you never need to read for more than thirty minutes without a break. Even reading complicated, technical or apparently 'dry' material will be a pleasure because the information will mean more to you.

Further reading the five-step way

To find the ideal books for *you*:

1. Get a clear idea of your desired *outcome* and the questions you need to answer to achieve it.
2. Visit a good bookshop. Find the section with books that might answer those questions.
3. Based on the cover and back page information, select books that may be relevant to your purpose.
4. Do steps one to four of the five-step system on each book.
5. Choose the books that have the relevant information and then decide which you want to invest in.

INSTANT TIP

Know your purpose! Why are you reading or dealing with a particular piece of information? What do you want to achieve by spending your time on it? If it has no value, put it aside.

06

How do you deal with verbal overload?

The difficulty with verbal information is that if you miss it, you miss it. You can rarely ask people to repeat what they say because you drifted off. But when too much information is coming at you too fast it's not so easy to stay focused, especially if the information isn't that interesting.

Perform at your best even when you are stressed with overload

Performance anxiety can happen in any situation where you have to perform: contributing to meetings with colleagues, speaking on stage in front of several thousand strangers, or sitting an exam. Regardless of the context, the symptoms of performance anxiety include clouded vision, blurred thinking, weak knees, excessive perspiration and weak lips to the extent that you think you would drool if you could summon up enough moisture. Then there is the activity in your head, concern whether your zips and buttons are fastened, if there is loo roll stuck to your shoe. These are symptoms of performance anxiety. Whatever, take a step back, breathe and relax.

Focusing on yourself and what your audience might be thinking about you, rather than what your audience needs and what you want to say to them, causes most performance anxiety and mental overload.

Consider these questions during preparation. The answers will help you generate the right attitude for a great performance:

- What do you want to have happen as a direct or indirect result of the material you will present?
- What message do you want your audience to receive?
- Have you imagined yourself in their place?
- What actions do you want them to take?
- What specific changes do you want to have happen as a result of your message?
- What response do you want from your audience *during* your message?
- What language is your audience accustomed to?
- What mood will your audience be in before, during and after you speak?
- What *other* messages might your audience be receiving at the same time as yours?
- What concerns might your audience have as a result of your message?
- What questions might your audience have?
- How will you present or deliver appropriately to reach out to everyone in the audience?

DO NOT think about yourself – your audience doesn't really care about you. What they want is the message. You are merely delivering it. If you think about yourself, you will be preoccupied with 'stuff' about which your audience has no interest. They want the message, then they want time and space to make decisions about it. They don't want to have to feel sorry for you. If that is what you want then that is all you will get, and they will not *listen* to what you have to *say*.

Adrenalin is good. It sharpens your thinking and your reactions. Fear undoes everything and increases the cortisol dose. Most audiences want to see a speaker succeed. Even if you speak to an audience that would prefer to shoot you down, the calmer you are, the less likely they are to succeed.

Preparation

A true story!

Several years ago I (*TK*) decided to break into a bigger market with a particular course I had been delivering to smaller clients. Three months before the event I booked a room at the premises of one of my key potential clients, at that time one of the world's biggest companies. I advertised the event – a free evening demonstration for new clients selected from all over the city. I then prepared the material – posters, handouts, business cards, course outlines, terms and conditions – organised a buffet and bar; you name it, I organised it. On the night about fifty new clients arrived. They included heads of training and sales agents that I intended would sell my course. They milled into the room, met each other, and then sat down in anticipation of the demonstration they had been promised. They had expectations. I stood up in front of my market place, a potentially large amount of very good work and realised that I had been so busy 'preparing' the *event* that I had forgotten to prepare what I would actually say. It was the most astounding piece of 'winging' I have ever done, but nowhere near as good as if I had got my priorities right and not got so caught up with non-core details. The event was not as successful as I had hoped it would be. I did learn one of the biggest lessons of my career: focus on your message.

Some tips about preparation

- First, prepare the message.
- Get to know your audience: find out as much about them as you can. The more you know about them the more at ease you will feel with them and they with you.
- Find out their concerns and address them early in your presentation: that will help them be more at ease with you.
- Keep your notes limited.
- Relax. Keep your audience in mind.
- Plan and do the 'adminis-trivia' for the event well in advance. Prepare a checklist to confirm that all is properly set up. Then forget about the administration and do the job of preparing your message.
- Do a dress rehearsal.

The loss of focus before or during a performance is usually due to lack of preparation. The frustrating thing about preparation is that the more time you have to prepare, the more time you have to generate fear. When preparing, prepare your mental attitude for the event as well as what you will say and do.

- When you speak, you *own* the space. Invite your audience into it. Your audience is there by your invitation.
- Really get to know and understand your message.
- Talk about your message to other people – not in the form of a prepared speech, rather in conversation.
- Be *passionate* about what you want to say. Excitement wins audiences. Period. It automatically focuses your mind on what you are saying instead of fears you might otherwise have had.

Things to avoid

Jokes

Don't include jokes in your presentations unless you:

- know the audience
- are absolutely sure that no one will be offended
- make the joke specific to them
- understand the audience culture: different companies and even departments within in the same company have different cultures – a joke that works for one legal firm might not work for another
- ensure a laughing start is appropriate
- have confidence in your ability to deliver the punch line successfully.

If you are concerned about your ability to deliver the joke at the start of your presentation, your follow through might suffer. Even good jokes will fail if you flummox the follow-up. *Never* tell a joke for the sake of it. An impromptu comment in keeping with the event has a better chance of making the audience smile than a joke you prepared weeks ago with no prior knowledge of the audience.

If you are in any doubt how a joke would be received, the simple rule is to leave jokes to professional comedians.

However ...

Laughter is important. It helps to generate a constructive atmosphere. A good honest laugh from you or the audience relieves tension, calms nerves, clears heads and helps audience bonding so that if you require them to interact in any way or ask questions, there is a greater likelihood that they will.

If you don't know the audience, have several openings prepared.

Don't stick to your plan too rigidly

If the needs of your audience change during the event, for instance, if they receive unexpected information that affects them, be flexible enough to change what you intend to say to blend with them. If a previous speaker has pre-empted part of what you had intended to say, adapt your material to suit. If a previous speaker has contradicted what you are going to say, respond appropriately to the contradiction. If you have something more interesting, include it.

However ...

Keep to the core of your message. Don't be influenced into changing *all* of what you intended to say by what someone else says. Get *your* message across.

Don't be tied down by notes

Audiences dislike being presented with the top of a speaker's head as he or she reads a carefully prepared essay word for word. Such speakers are afraid of being distracted by the audience and losing their place. Reading from an essay bores an audience because the lack of eye contact prevents them from interacting with the speaker. Compared with speaking and communicating directly with the audience, the tone of voice while reading is impersonal and monotonous. Also, when a speaker reads a pre-prepared speech, they do not think!

However ...

If you are worried about notes there are other, more effective, ways of prompting yourself though the speech.

- Use a spider-graph. These are excellent for providing all the information you need, on one page, in colour. The good thing about working from a spider-graph is that you can be interrupted any number of times and you will not lose the place.
- When you build your spider-graph, make provisions for using overhead, flip-chart or computer presentation systems. These will prompt you as you speak at the same time as building a picture of what you say for your audience. This will keep them interested and involved. *Avoid* bullet point after bullet point written out so that all you do is read from the screen. They will be justifiably bored and irritated. They are, after all, able to read faster than you can speak.
- Know your subject well enough so that you only need a few words to remind you of what you want to say. Then you can speak fluently from genuine knowledge.
- Use your audience to build your speech. If you intend to answer audience questions, converse with the audience and find out their questions beforehand. Structure what you say around the questions gathered. This lets you remove rhetoric and get to the point. Your audience will appreciate that.
- Use imagination. If you must use essays, write a good one in preparation, then summarise it in a spider-graph.

Don't get your audience to join in too early

If you speak to a general audience – especially a large one – avoid asking for audience responses at the very start of your presentation without carefully thinking about a strategy for ensuring a response. Most audiences are lazy. They want to hear what you have to say and for you to create a good atmosphere in which they will happily participate, if they choose to.

However ...

The more you involve your audience, the easier it will be for them to accept difficult information, ask questions or join in later. Most people are nervous about speaking out in public and would prefer not to speak from the audience. The same performance anxieties apply whether you speak from your seat in the audience or from the stage. So when you ask for comments from the audience, especially if they were not pre-warned, don't be surprised at the lack of volunteers.

Involvement technique

1. Before the audience arrives, put flip-chart pens at their seats and pin large pieces of paper on the walls. Put up enough paper for two to ten people to work at each sheet.
2. Draw a vertical line down the middle of each sheet. At the top of the left side write the heading, 'What do you already know about (your subject)?' and on the other half write, 'What questions do you have about (your subject)?'
3. Get the audience to answer these two questions at the start of your presentation. Avoid 'fancy' introductions. The sooner they speak among themselves and ask each other questions, the more involved and interested they will be in the material you present.
4. When you give instructions specify two rules: 1) they can't say 'nothing' on the 'what do you know' side and 2) they must fill the page with normal sized print (the reason for this is that they will try harder – if you tell them to write only a couple of points down, they will literally write two points).
5. While they are filling the sheets, go and meet each group, speak to them, get them to explain and discuss their questions. This will create a noise in the room. A buzz.
6. When they have no more questions, seat them. Tell them that they will, at the end of the presentation, have the opportunity to check that their questions have all been answered.

The aim is to get them to speak up without having to stand out. I use the involvement technique described above at most events. It has worked every time so far. It works particularly well if you are speaking about a technical subject or teaching a new skill.

This strategy does several things:

1. The audience interacts with you and with each other.
2. You can discover how much they know already and what they need to know.
3. It generates a relaxed, safe environment (no one feels forced to stand out).
4. It makes the event relevant to the audience. This will help you gain their attention.
5. When you ask, 'Does anyone have any questions?' at the end of the presentation, you won't be met with silence because your audience will have already gathered all the questions they want answered and are, at this stage, accustomed to contributing.
6. Because you know their questions from the outset, you will know whether you have answered them successfully.
7. The audience will appreciate that the information you present will benefit them and you will gain their trust.

Working with the audience

Have you noticed changes in tone, body language, attitude and performance of a speaker when their presentation ends and they take questions? They relax, they think before they speak, they slow and vary their pace, they become more interesting and interested and they are more animated. Which do you prefer: answering questions or presenting your material uninterrupted?

Don't apologise at the beginning

Never start a presentation with 'I'm not going to bore you for long', 'Sorry if I seem nervous but I am' or 'I'll be quick so someone more interesting can speak'. If you want sympathy, go to someone who cares. It's brutal, but true. Your audience does not care. In fact, when you start a presentation saying how boring or nervous you are, you will lose most of your audience. They do not want to listen to someone make excuses. Telling the audience will not make your nerves go away. And if you truly believe that you bore your audience, why speak at all?

However ...

No, however. Just get on with it. If the subject is boring, *make it interesting*. If you are passionate, boredom and nerves will disappear.

Speaking in meetings

Contributing to a meeting is just as much *performance* as delivering a speech. In each case you are trying to transmit a message. During a meeting it is easy to say the first thing that comes into your head instead of saying what you *mean* to say. It is equally easy to say nothing to avoid saying something 'stupid'.

Keep your head clear during meetings. Most people have an agenda of their own and there is almost always internal politics. To respond successfully during meetings:

- Think before you speak.
- As the meeting progresses, take notes to remind you of your thoughts.
- Don't be bullied into responding to comments or suggestions.
- Don't let anyone threaten you, emotionally, physically, intellectually or psychologically.
- Stick to the facts and don't get emotional.

Impromptu speeches: seven steps in seven minutes

For most people, a prepared speech and contributing at meetings are easy compared with being asked to give an impromptu speech. One of two things may fill your mind when you are asked to speak with no notice: first, nothing at all, your mind goes totally blank; second, mental overdrive. To prevent either mental block, relax and clear your head using one of the relaxation techniques in Chapter 2. Then, use the following strategy to create a structure around which to build a clear and balanced speech.

Step 1: 30 seconds
Calm down, breathe and focus your mind on the specific topic you will be speaking about.

Step 2: 30 seconds
On a piece of paper, write the title of your speech in one clear sentence.

Step 3: 1 minute
Either as a spider-graph or linearly, write between three and six main topics you will want to cover during your speech (if you are being asked to speak without notice it is unlikely you will have to speak for long – four points will generally be enough).

Step 4: 1 minute
Write two sub-points for each of the main topics.

Step 5: 2 minutes
Briefly develop each point.

Step 6: 1 minute
Write a conclusion.

Step 7: 1 minute
Write an introduction.

For a two-minute speech on 'Information Overload', the process would be something like this:

Step 1: Breathe, relax and clear your mind.

Step 2: Write 'Information Overload' on a piece of a paper.

Step 3: Four key points on information overload:
- Definition of information overload
- Reasons for information overload
- Main challenges when trapped by information overload
- How to avoid information overload and create balance

Step 4: Two sub-points for each of the key points:
- Definition of information overload
  - Mental switch from order to chaos
  - Perception
- Reasons for information overload
  - Perfectionism
  - Denial
- Main challenges when trapped by information overload
  - Stress
  - Consequences of inaction
- How to avoid information overload and create balance
  - Work/life balance
  - Regaining perspective

Step 5: Build each point by adding detail to each of the above sub-points

Step 6: Write your conclusion by briefly summarising the key points.

Step 7: Write your introduction by outlining the main topics you will be speaking about.

Remember, if you feel unqualified to speak on a subject at short notice, say so.

Ten tips on performing under pressure

1. Slow down. Think of your audience.
2. Have a clear message.
3. Stick to the point. Avoid waffle.
4. Make the presentation relevant. Find out what the audience knows before you start.
5. Speak from knowledge instead of notes.
6. Don't embarrass your audience by asking them to do something they don't want to do.
7. Enjoy it. It's not often you have a group of people prepared to sit and listen to you without interrupting.
8. Take control of your space quickly and confidently.
9. Look and sound confident.
10. Be firm. Don't allow rude or abusive behaviour.

What if you were the world authority on your subject? How would your demeanour, attitude, body language, tone and dress change? How would you treat your audience differently? How interested would your audience be in your subject if you were truly interested?

INSTANT TIP

The failure or success of a presentation is determined by the speaker's attitude to their subject *and* their audience.

07

How do you avoid overloading other people?

'Do to others as you want them to do to you' is a good philosophy when it comes to distributing information. Consider the workload of others: how do they like to receive information? What is the most effective and efficient way of dealing with that individual?

Instead of white-washing your colleagues with irrelevant information, take a moment to consider what they really need. This, after all, is how you'd like them to treat you.

How to avoid being an information bottleneck

Having too much to read every day causes pressure at work. If you have more to read than you have time for, the reason might be either:

- the need to know everything
- procrastination.

Do you read *everything* that crosses your desk because you are worried that if you don't, you won't be able to do your job or help others do theirs?

'Needing to know everything' is a controlling attitude. It frustrates colleagues and turns a desk into a bottleneck. Some of the symptoms are:

- **Apparent urgency:** dealing with something as soon as you receive it no matter what else has to be done or how important it is in comparison to other things. If someone gives you a document to read and says, 'This is urgent, you must read it now', don't take their word for it. Although it may be urgent according to others, in your schedule of priorities it might be second or third. Prioritise *your* time.
- **Nobody does it better:** excellent attitude if you want to work every weekend and most holidays. Most people are capable of doing their jobs well. Think lucky, have faith, prioritise and delegate.
- **Generosity:** You cannot always afford to be generous with your time. Often the people giving you something extra to deal with may be avoiding doing it themselves.

Don't accept anything that lands on your desk unless you know:

- that you are the best person to process the information
- why you should read it
- what you are expected to do with it.

Procrastination is another reason excess reading material accumulates. Two causes of procrastination are fear or lack of interest. If a task seems challenging you might do other seemingly important things instead of dealing with reality.

The cure is straightforward. Instead of imagining how bad a task might be, determine precisely what it entails. Get the facts. Then chunk the work into do-able pieces. Then do one piece at a time.

If the cause is lack of interest, find something about it that motivates you. If you find nothing and your desk is always full of paperwork but you just can't be bothered, consider negotiating your job description. Or find a different job!

Being a bottleneck achieves little. Information must flow freely in an organisation. You will be surprised how much you can achieve when you enlist the help of others and share information.

Paper fatigue

When you have so much unread material that you begin to feel as though you cannot cope, you experience 'paper fatigue': a sense of exhaustion when you go near your desk. This has more to do with perception than with reality. The more effectively you prioritise and organise reading, the faster you get through it. New information becomes manageable.

How to prioritise and organise reading?

● put time aside
● do the five-step process on your in-tray every day.

INSTANT TIP

Take time to prepare all outgoing information. That means that you will send out less because you are spending more time on quality rather than quantity.

08

How do you remember what you need to remember?

Overload produces tension. One of the first mental faculties to suffer under pressure is your memory, a great memory.

This chapter will provide techniques on how to:

- remember what you need to remember, when you need to remember it
- keep a clear head in stressful environments
- remember the people you meet
- be creative and recall relevant information under pressure.

Maintaining a good memory

Memory is key to everything we do: meeting people, learning new information, planning your day. With so much practice, our memories should be excellent. Instead, many complain that not only is their memory not good enough, it's getting worse!

The good news ...

1. Developing a strong, reliable memory is easy.
2. You don't have to practise complicated mnemonics.
3. The more relaxed you are the better your memory will become. So roll out the yoga mat and book a massage!

A good memory is one of the best signals that you are not suffering from overload. If you are stressed, frustrated, angry, fearful or bogged down with life, your memory will suffer. You may be forgetting names, appointments, conversations or what someone just told you a moment ago.

Rather than the amount of information being the major contributing factor to memory difficulties, it is our attitude towards it.

Memory principles

- Memory is not a stand-alone system; it relies on attention, perception and reasoning.
- Memory is not a system based on isolated facts. Everything you remember is interconnected to other information in memory.
- Memory retrieval relies greatly on association. The better organised you are, the more organised your memory will be and the easier it will be to recall information.
- New information is not stored separately from old information. Old knowledge helps make sense of new

information and vice versa (one reason why it is easier to read material you know something about).

- Memory is not only for storing information, it is designed for use.
- We speak about memory as if it were an object. We describe ourselves as having a 'good', 'bad' or 'average' memory, in the same way as 'good' or 'bad' lungs. Your memory is not a *thing*. It is certainly not a *single* thing. It is a series of processes taking place in your brain, all the time.
- Your memory can be trained. It has been said that there are no good or bad memories, just trained or untrained. Barring organic damage, with few exceptions, everyone's memory can be developed.
- One common excuse for not wanting to improve memory is, 'I'm too old!!!' If your mind and body are healthy, age is no excuse.
- The more you use your memory the stronger it will become. Many memory problems that people encounter as they become older are due to lack of mental exercise, lack of physical exercise, poor nutrition and excess stress.
- A basic guideline for improving memory and ability to concentrate is to focus on physical and mental health: what is good for the body is also good for the mind.
- A major factor in memory failure is stress.
- Memory includes long-term memory, short-term memory, very short-term memory, kinaesthetic memory, recall, retrieval, recognition, storage ... If any one part of this process is not functioning well, your memory, will be working below optimum. There is little point absorbing material without a retrieval mechanism.
- One final fallacy is that by memorising too much, you will fill up your brain.

Before we discuss improving your memory, consider how your memory works.

Short-term, intermediate and long-term memory

Short-term memory holds information for seconds and then it is lost. Without short-term memory every piece of information you see, hear, smell, touch or taste would be instantaneously remembered and accessible. This could make gathering new information very difficult. If you want what is in your short-term memory to be available for later recall, you have to pay attention to it and take action to remember it for a longer period of time.

Intermediate memory is retained for typically two to four hours. Have you ever decided to remember something interesting, and then several hours later have not been able to recall what it was? This is intermediate memory. As soon as information is no longer required, it is discarded. This is one reason why you forget people's names. You meet them once, they are remembered while you see them. After the event you might not think about them for a while. Next time you meet them, because your visual memory is stronger than your auditory memory, you might remember where you met them and what they were wearing, but you may not be able to recall their name.

Long-term memory is what people complain about most often. In reading, for instance, your short-term memory retains information long enough for you to make sense of the sentence or paragraph you are reading. Intermediate memory retains information long enough so that you can make sense of the chapter. Long-term memory helps you remember and make sense of the whole book. Long-term memory requires revision and application.

Long-term memory works with short-term and intermediate memory. As you might imagine, the three systems are interconnected. Gaps or weaknesses in one of them will prevent the whole system from working effectively.

How memory works – and when it doesn't – a simple model

There are many models that attempt to explain how the memory system works. Basically, your memory is divided into three parts:

- **Acquisition** – absorbing information via sensation, perception and interpretation
- **Retention** – keeping it in your head
- **Retrieval** – getting it out again.

A memory can become unavailable at any point. The trouble is, you only know it is unavailable when you try to retrieve it: you are in the company of someone whose name you have forgotten, unable to introduce them to someone (whose name you have also forgotten!).

There are some basic rules that will help you improve your memory:

Four steps to memory acquisition

Pay attention

Most of the time you 'forget' something because you deprived yourself of the opportunity to remember it in the first place. Have you ever been introduced to someone then several seconds later you realised you had 'forgotten' their name? Chances are your attention was somewhere else – you were not present.

Plan

Before you begin, think forward to when you will be likely to use the information. In what context will you use it? What state will you be in (calm, excited, nervous) when you want the information (exam conditions for instance)?

Be interested

Even if the event seems dull, find something in or about it that interests you. If you are bored, parts of your brain will not be involved and this will make paying attention even more difficult.

Be active

Think about what you are doing. Your memory does not work in isolation. The more connections you make between the new and old information the easier it will be to understand and integrate. Understanding and integration are key to remembering.

Memory retention (storage)

Storing information in your head is one thing, storing it in such a way that you can retrieve it later is a different matter.

Your memory thrives on association and order. The better organised your memory, the easier it will be to retrieve information when you need it. You do not have to keep everything in your head. Be organised on paper and you will know where to find the information when you need it.

Memory needs rehearsal and revision so that it may be effectively retained and recalled. There are several ways to achieve this. The least effective is rote rehearsal: as soon as the memory is interfered with, the information disappears. For instance – if someone gives you a telephone number and then asks where you put your keys, the telephone number will fade. The loss of the keys, will take your mind on a search. You will be attending to that instead of trying to store the number.

The more mental time you spend on thinking about and understanding what you are trying to remember the better chance you will have of remembering it.

Memory retrieval

Memories are stored in several parts of your brain. When you recall your memory of your front door, several areas of your brain will be activated. You might simultaneously:

- see an internal picture of your door (visual)
- hear the sound of it closing (auditory)
- recall the last time you walked through it (kinaesthetic and proprioceptive)
- remember the feeling of the last time you locked yourself out (emotional)
- smell the fresh coat of paint when you painted it last (olfactory).

When we try to retrieve information we often use only one access point. If you can re-create the whole experience as you remembered it, it will be easier for you to recall further information. One reason we have difficulty retrieving information is that the retrieval method is inappropriate.

Depending on how the information was originally presented to you, there are different types of memory retrieval. The easiest information to remember is information you can easily recognise and fit into an existing schema or framework. Recognising a face is sometimes easier than remembering the name that goes with it. When you are looking for information you have read previously you might say that you know where it is, you can see it on the page and when you find the page, you recognise the text, you just cannot recall the actual piece of information itself.

Recall is when you are given no clues at all. As opposed to *recognising* a face, you have to *recall* their name. Most information that you forget is the information you have to recall.

Forgetting

We often become aware of our memories only when we forget something. Memory failure can happen because of disorganisation, distraction or lack of awareness.

Studying the difficulties that people have when recalling information can help us understand how our memories work. Memories are often available (we know we have read it, or seen it, we can remember where we were when we remembered it in the first place) but the actual information is not accessible (just cannot quite remember it fully). This phenomenon is called 'tip of the tongue'. Most psychologists think that long-term memory is organised in categories, and these categories are linked, much like a spider-graph. One thing reminds you of the next and so on. If these links change or become damaged in any way then the information might become inaccessible. You might forget it entirely. 'Forget' in this sense means that you are unable to reconstruct the information.

Factors contributing to forgetfulness

Lack of attention (the pickpocket effect)

Problem: If you pay full attention to a task, you will not notice other things going on around you. While it might seem like a contradiction, daydreaming is one of the few activities we carry out with full attention. Next time you notice your mind wander, notice how much of your surroundings you were paying attention to. Did you notice the normal noise around you or see people moving about?

Workaround: Improve your concentration. Chapter 5 can help you with this.

Interference

Problem: Interference can be retroactive or proactive. When you change your telephone number the new one somehow 'latches' onto your memory and replaces the old one. This is called *retroactive interference.* It comes from new information. *Proactive interference* is when old information interferes with new information. Thinking of your telephone number again, this is when you cannot remember your new one because your old number keeps coming into your mind instead.

Workaround: To work around retroactive and proactive interference, rest between different stages or pieces of work. This allows time for your mind to consolidate new information, to separate old information and integrate new information within the framework of your existing knowledge (unless it is your telephone number).

Lack of interest or motivation

Problem: Remembering new information is almost impossible without interest or some motivation. Tiredness can contribute to this. Even if you are interested in what you are working on, the interest will fade if you are tired.

Workaround: Find something that motivates you, no matter how small or seemingly unrelated. The task must benefit you in some way or another. Take breaks as often as you feel you need them – at least ten to fifteen minutes every hour to hour and a half.

Insufficient links or association

Problem: If the information or job is particularly new to you, making sense of the ideas may be challenging due to your framework being in the early stage of development. If you cannot make sense of the ideas you will find them very difficult to remember.

Workaround: Study the glossary of terminology and any other related topics. This will help develop the mental infrastructure. For example, become familiar with the legends and conversions of a road map or atlas before using a map.

Insufficient revision

Problem: Memories are made of memory traces. If they are not reinforced they will fade.

Workaround: A basic guideline is to revise seven times in ten days, or develop a very good filing system. To remember information in the long-term, use it or lose it.

Stress and memory

Stress destroys memory. Period. When you are stressed you release high levels of the hormone cortisol into your body. Cortisol affects you in a variety of ways depending on the amount released into your body. Cortisol destroys glucose, your brain's *only* source of food.

If you have ever been involved in or witnessed an accident or other trauma, you may have 'got through it', and appeared to be fully conscious. Afterwards you may have been unable to remember anything, or had an inadequate memory about the incident. You would have experienced a level of stress that caused the release of a large amount of cortisol which would have affected the hippocampus area of your brain and destroyed the glucose. With no food your brain literally did not have the necessary materials to lay the long-term memory down. You saw everything. Maybe even walked around and spoke to people. But the memories were not laid down in any form that can be recalled.

It is even more complex than that. If the hormones go into the same configuration at the time of the event, a phenomenon known as 'state dependent memory' can cause flashbacks and behavioural or mood problems. So the memory does get laid down but not in a way that is ordinarily readily available. If you experience such problems after a trauma there are several therapeutic approaches that may help.

A less extreme effect happens if, for example, you are about to give a speech, meet new people, introduce your boss to your partner. You might feel a little fuzziness or other sensation. You know that you know what you should know, but you can't quite get the ideas, names or words correct. It might feel somewhat like a telephone line in a storm. The lines are there, communication should be possible, but there's interference from somewhere.

There is a further scenario in which cortisol affects your brain and is damaging in a different way. People who live a highly stressed life have a self-induced, intravenous drip of cortisol into their bodies. This cortisol destroys glucose and turns calcium into free radicals that destroy brain cells. This can cause age-related memory loss. People between age forty and fifty years might feel that they're not thinking as fast and clearly as they once did. Left unchecked these consequences can be permanent. No matter what age you are (and providing there is no organic damage to your memory), or what myth you choose to believe, your memory *will* become clearer, more creative, more active and more accurate if you work at it.

Although there will be no overnight effect, constant and determined action will be rewarded. There is no magic pill for instant memory. If you choose to be, you have the natural capacity to be brilliant. It takes effort, common sense and belief in yourself.

In summary, pressure makes it difficult to remember. The first step to developing a great memory is learning how to cope with stress in situations where you need to remember.

De-stress when you need to remember

Factors that contribute to your stress levels are:

- the amount of information you need to remember
- the time you have available
- your control over the situation
- your confidence in your ability to recall.

When you feel stressed, say 'STOP!' very loudly in your head. Imagine everything around you freezes to a standstill, then take a mental or physical step backwards. Then:

1. Smile, breathe deeply twice (abdominally), stand or sit up straight.
2. Inside your head (or out loud) laugh. A real belly laugh is a superb de-stresser.
3. Ask those around you to slow down.
4. Take your time to answer questions and speak just a little more slowly.
5. Write information down if it's appropriate.

Remember names and faces

One strategy for remembering the names and faces of those you meet is to **prepare**, **pay attention** and **practise**:

Prepare

Before an event: get the agenda and a guest list, study it and look for names of people who you have met and know well, people you think you have met but can't remember clearly and people you want to meet. Then prepare a strategy for who you are going to meet first. If you want to see the people you know well first, then when you walk into the room, look for the person you want to speak to and go directly to them without making eye contact with anyone else. This will prevent you being ambushed by too many new faces as soon as you arrive and will give you time to become familiar with the room. The best way to gain control is to arrive early to meet the people you want to meet, one at a time.

Pay attention

When two people meet for the first time, natural first impressions happen within the first few seconds. However, while the first impression is developing, you are also being introduced and by the time you introduce yourself, you often realise you didn't catch their name because you didn't hear it. You didn't hear it because your attention was elsewhere.

The first time you meet someone:

- Smile, breathe slowly and abdominally, and take your time.
- Spend enough time with each person you meet (if possible).
- Listen carefully to the name. Say it back to make sure you are pronouncing it correctly.
- Ask the spelling, especially if it's a difficult name or if the person mumbled.
- If the event allows, stick to first names only.
- Pay attention to the whole person: their style of dress, postures, gestures, unique identifying features and how they walk.
- Get a business card.
- Then ...

Practise

- *Use* people's names. Help them by using yours. If you have forgotten their name, ask for it, people will not be offended. If you think they will be, ask someone else for it.
- If someone struggles to remember your name, use it in the conversation '... and I said to myself, Tina, ...'.
- Introduce yourself when you join a group. Don't wait for someone else to do it; they might not.
- Finally, get into the habit of making the introductions.

Ten tips on how to develop a great memory

1. Be present – listen and pay attention to what is going on around you. Most forgetting is the result of not remembering in the first place.
2. During a meeting, keep your mind clear by listening instead of constructing your reply. Write down beforehand what you want to say.
3. Good eating habits, plenty of exercise, a relaxed attitude and sufficient sleep all go a long way to improving your memory. Ginkgo biloba, ginseng and lecithin may help too.
4. The more you use what you want to remember, the easier it will be to recall later.
5. Make yourself memorable by introducing yourself slowly and clearly.
6. The more background information you know about something, the easier it will be to recall. Whether it's about a subject or a person, ask questions about what you want to know.
7. Good focus and concentration is key to good memory.
8. If possible, do one thing at a time.
9. Stick to habits. If you always put your keys in one place, you are unlikely to lose them.
10. Don't be too stressed if you happen to forget something.

A thought

Imagine ... Walking along the beach, you feel the warm sand between your toes. The warmth on your feet, sand slipping under your soles, reminds you of a holiday you took three years ago – the people you met, the fun, the beach party ... Is the memory in your mind? Or is it in your toes?

INSTANT TIP

You are human. Don't beat yourself up if you forget something. Look instead at why you might have forgotten it and solve the problem from the root cause, up.

09

How do you learn without overload?

If you are working and studying at the same time it is important that what you want to achieve is achievable and consistent with your other commitments. It is easy to be so absorbed in the extra work that you forget the time you need to spend with your family and friends. If you work and study and don't give yourself enough Quality Recovery Time (rest and play) your stress levels will increase and your effectiveness will decrease – thus defeating the entire object. The popular study subjects don't tend to be the informal ones that are flexible with working hours but the kind of study programmes that have deadlines, exams and are for many people a substitute for a life at some times of the year.

In this chapter we will look at what taking a typical course (e.g. MBA or Open University course) entails and what you can do to make life easier, productive and successful.

Before you begin

Whether you are going into the first, second or third year of a course, there are some crucial things to think about before you begin:

Available time

Do you honestly have the time to do the course justice? Most of us will say 'no' but do it anyway. If that is the case then make sure that your reasons for doing the course are solid. Whatever your reasons are, make sure that you can at least put some time aside. Try to make study time a set time of the day. Start putting that time aside for a month or so before you begin the course. This will give your family time to adjust to your new routine and will allow you to become used to taking that time to sit quietly and focus your mind by doing some preparatory reading.

Tip

If time is *really* a problem and you *have* to do the course, limit the amount of time you spend on each session. Rather spend thirty minutes every day and then several hours at a weekend or evening than spend no time at all during the week and a whole day on Saturday or Sunday. Little and often – like a healthy diet.

Access to resources

Do you have access to all the resources you are going to need? Are you a member of the nearest library? Do you need to become a member of a university library? They often have texts that an ordinary library won't have. Do you know people you could speak to and discuss issues with? Make contact with any appropriate lecturers and study the Internet.

Family and friends support

Get your family involved. You need their support for two reasons: first, to give you the space and time to work, and second, to push you along when you are feeling a little demotivated (which will happen from time to time). If you have children, teach them to speed-read and use pictures, books or ideas from your course so that they know exactly what you are doing. Get your partner involved as well if he/she wants to be. When you get your timetable of the year ahead, put it on the fridge door so that everyone can see what you are committed to.

Desire and purpose

Make sure you know exactly why you are doing this. What is the pay-off? Is it big enough to compensate for the weekend reading you will have to do?

Pre-course preparation

During the month before you start, gather information that will help you during the course, revise notes from previous courses and read other related material. During this time you can also set up a good filing system for your assignments and reading materials. Build spider-graphs or index cards of everything you already know and, every day, list at least five questions you are going to want to answer throughout the course. Also, on a daily basis tell yourself why you are taking the course. If you keep saying, 'I don't know' then reassess whether you should continue or not.

Break down the course

The week you get your first course materials is very important. One of the mistakes people make is to read only what they have to read when they are told they should read it. To fully benefit from every piece of reading and work you do, follow these steps:

1. Read your list of assignments first and, if you can get hold of past exam papers, do so.
2. Once you have had a look at what assignments you have to deliver, follow the five-step system and go through the first four steps from *Prepare* (which you would have been doing for the past month) to *Active* reading. Do this for *all* the books, articles and papers you have. As you read, take thorough notes of what you find interesting, what looks challenging, what seems to be familiar and what is totally new to you. Always keep in mind the assignments you will have to complete.
3. Next, go through the list of questions you have built up over the month before the course. Answer those you can and add more to the list.
4. Try to make a first pass though all of your course material within the first week of your course.
5. Then, study your timetable, determine what has to be studied by when and break down your reading into the smallest possible chunks.

Tip

When you design your timetable, don't make every day a study day. Try to keep two days per week free of course work. This is for Quality Recovery Time and in case something happens on one of the designated study days and you miss a session. It is also a good idea to be at least a week ahead of your course. There will be time when you miss several reading sessions in a row and having to catch up will put on pressure, increasing your stress levels unnecessarily. Take the time at the start of the course to plan – it will be the best time spent.

Save time

Preparing for more than one assignment at a time

Although most assignments are on different subjects within your course, these subjects will all be somehow related. When you are doing the research for one assignment always find out what the next one or two are about. You will be able to save a lot of time by keeping future assignments in mind and if you come across an idea or section of text that would be useful for future assignments, write it down with a note explaining why you thought it was a good idea and what made you think of it in the first place, including any page numbers and book titles. Then, file it in the system you developed before the course began.

Preparing for the exam from the start of the course

Another mistake people make is to leave any thought of studying for the exam until right at the end of the course. If you start preparing for the exam at the beginning of the course and keeping the exam in mind as you write and submit essays and projects – instead of panicking about the exam a week before – you will have several weeks before the exam for stress-free revision.

Revise

The more revision you do as you go, the easier the course will be. When you begin to revise for an exam, few things are more frustrating than the discovery that everything is unfamiliar to you even though you know you have already read it and perhaps even written an assignment on it.

Make it a habit to revise every day. At the start of each session spend twenty minutes going over past notes, spider-graphs and index cards refreshing your memory. As you do this, link in different ideas and add new thoughts to your growing collection of knowledge. The more you can integrate your thinking the more natural revision will become. If you revise a little every day all you need to do for the exam is to review your notes (much like you have done every day since the start of the course) and add new thoughts or ideas to an already thorough body of knowledge (to make this easier, double space your notes so that you have the space to add clear comments later).

Preparation for an exam when you have stuck to your study plan

If you have managed to structure your course and if you have revised daily and begun to prepare for the exam at the start of the course instead of waiting till the end, you will be fully prepared and ready to sit a successful exam.

Preparation for an exam when you have NOT stuck to your study plan

If you have not had time to structure your course or if you are reading this book and you are halfway through a course already, there is a way to make sure you are able to sit the exam confidently. The following points will help you structure your reading so that you succeed without causing yourself undue stress:

- Determine how many study days you have before the exam or end of the course. Be realistic about this. If you are working full time as well as studying, then remember that you will only have mornings, evenings and weekends and that you have to fit a life in there somewhere.
- Establish exactly what you have to study. If you gather all the material you will be able to see that the amount of information you have to learn is finite. This does your morale good if nothing else.
- Go through the course timetable and notes and make a list of all the different areas you have to cover.

- Under each heading write down the chapters, tapes, videos, CDs, DVDs, downloads and lectures (*all* sources) you have to refer to for information.
- Organise the headings in an 'information order'. Some areas of a subject serve as good background for others so cover those first. The order in which you study these areas is entirely up to you and will depend on your current knowledge base.
- Once all areas are covered, you have identified the sources for each area; put them in sequence and create a realistic and achievable timetable – remember QRT (Quality Recovery Time).
- The timetable you create should not have you starting at 4 a.m. and beginning again as soon as you get home – you will burn out. Make space in your timetable for Quality Recovery Time (QRT). Have plenty of it.
- Create a good space, that, if possible should only be used for study.
- Enjoy the learning process by rewarding yourself for each accomplishment (at least one a day). Choose ways that don't run up your dental bills or medical visits. Try cycling, a walk in the hills, swimming or a piece of fruit. Avoid chocolate or coffee, but if that is what you want, make sure it is of the highest quality.

If you are studying and working at the same time the most important thing is to have a clear objective, a clear purpose and as much support as you can muster – and most important of all, ENJOY IT and have fun!

Team up

Part of what I (*TK*) do is teach students accelerated learning techniques. One student was having particular difficulty. His exam was getting closer and he couldn't settle down to study. After trying everything from learning map techniques to attending extra lectures and individual tuition from his lecturers he was considering giving up. We thought, however, that instead of throwing in the towel he should try one more thing.

At the end of a series of courses on learning skills all the delegates choose a subject they are interested in, do the research on it and then teach the rest of the class. This student focused on his course work. We thought that if he tried to teach others what he was trying to learn he might be able to find the gaps in his understanding of the subject. So he began to prepare for the session he was going to teach. When he gave the talk, several things happened. First, he enjoyed talking about the subject, second, people in the group asked him questions and he was able to answer them, and third, he realised that he learns best when he is showing someone else how to do it and has to prepare for it.

As a result, he got a group of colleagues together, split up the work between them, each of them studied their designated chapters and they got together every two days to teach what they had learned to the others.

He sat the exam and passed comfortably with a high band pass.

In brief

● Make sure you have the time, resources, support and desire before you commit yourself to studying and working at the same time.

● Prepare for the course before you begin.

● Get your family, friends and colleagues involved.

● Save time by thinking ahead as you study.

● Break down your course into manageable chunks.

● Start reading all of the course material from the start of the course to provide you with a 'big picture' of what the course entails. This will help to make sense of what you are doing.

● Revise regularly.

● Enjoy it.

Use your brain

One reason why learning can be difficult and the results short-lived is that most people do not give their brain everything it needs to make sense of and store new information. There are six stages to effective learning (see below). At school, most students only apply three of the six: Stage 2 (information intake – although it is more like in*put*), part of Stage 4 (memorise) and Stage 5 (demonstrate – not always successfully). As a result, many students suffer from post-performance amnesia – they write the exam and promptly forget everything they have learned. Unfortunately, because most people don't think there is a better way to learn, this style stays with them through tertiary education and into their careers. As a result, many people lack confidence when they have to learn something new (job, language, technology) because, if learning is anything like at school, they feel they don't have the skills to do it successfully.

If you follow *all* six stages of learning, new information will quickly become a useful part of your knowledge base.

Six stages of effective learning

Stage 1: Prepare

a. Develop a state of relaxed awareness. To achieve this, stretch your body and breathe deeply. Imagine your whole body relaxing from your toes to your head. When you reach your head imagine your brain filling with alert energy.

b. Focus on your subject and ask yourself:
   i. what you *already know*
   ii. what you *need* to know
   iii. what your *purpose* is
   iv. when and in what way will you will *use* the information.

c. Determine all the different sources of information available to you: books, people, video, journals, media, etc.

Stage 2: Information intake

a. Ask as many questions as you can about the subject.

b. Use the five-step reading system outlined in Chapter 1 to go through all written material.

c. Build spider-graphs; use colours and images.

d. Gather information from as many different sources as you can: video and audio, conversations, lectures, the Internet, etc.

Stage 3: Explore and expand

a. When you have learned the basics, begin to explore the new information by asking further questions and looking at the new knowledge from different perspectives.

b. Speak to people who know *nothing* about the subject and encourage them to ask questions.

c. Speak to professionals on the subject and ask even more questions.

Stage 4: Understand and memorise

a. When you have the facts, study them until you understand them. At school, it may have been acceptable simply to memorise key information. Few examiners want to trick their students. Their questions are fairly straightforward. At work however, your knowledge cannot be *re*-productive (repeating old information) it has to be *pro*ductive (able to generate new and original ideas); this requires an understanding of the subject.

b. The better you understand what you are learning, the easier it will be to apply it in different situations and remember long term.

Stage 5: Demonstrate

a. Find any excuse to demonstrate what you know: speak to the walls or your goldfish if no one will listen.

b. Write essays and speeches.

c. Apply new ideas.

Stage 6: Reflect

a. Think about what you have learned.

b. How else could you use it?

c. What changes will this new knowledge create in your life?

As a child you used all six stages automatically. You were curious, determined, excited and focused. You didn't give up. You asked 'why' questions and persevered until you got an answer. You explored alternatives. You were open to all possibilities. You didn't contemplate failure. You didn't limit your potential. You believed that learning was perfectly natural.

Walt Whitman said it perfectly in his poem, 'There Was a Child Went Forth':

> There was a child went forth every day,
> And the first object he look'd upon, that object he became,
> And that object became part of him for the day or a certain
>   part of the day,
> Or for many years or stretching cycles of years.

Your ability to learn has not changed; your attitude and belief in that ability may have.

If you learn about your mind and your ideal learning environment you will develop the skills to manipulate your internal and external environment to make learning easier and more effective.

Learn to suit your brain

The brain is divided into three main areas. If you hold your right hand in a fist and cover the top of your fist with your left hand, you will have an idea of what it looks like.

'Reptilian' brain

Your wrist represents your reptilian brain. This is the oldest part of your brain. When you were conceived, it was the first to develop. All animals have this basic brain. It keeps you alive.

Any form of physical harm or threat – intellectual, emotional, cultural-social or resource restriction – alerts your reptilian brain. To function efficiently it needs a safe environment, clear information, consideration, time, peripheral stimulation and freedom of choice. The reptilian brain's response to stress is flight, fight or freeze.

'Mammalian' brain

Your fist represents your limbic system. It is also called your 'mammalian brain' because all mammals have this brain. Among other things, it contains your hippocampus, which is responsible for memory, data retrieval and storage, your thalamus, which is responsible for attention, and the amygdala, which is responsible for emotion and pleasure.

To learn, the limbic system needs:

- **Emotion:** It is easier to learn and remember what you are passionate about. Remembering someone you like or don't like is easier than remembering someone you feel neutral about.
- **Convincing:** If you believe something to be true, it will be easier to remember and learn.
- **Multi-sensory input:** The more senses you use to absorb new information, the easier it will be to recall at a later date.
- **Revision:** Not just rote revision to memorise facts. Revise with the aim of fully understanding and integrating the new information.
- **Demonstration:** Show that you know.

To learn, the limbic system needs: colour, stories and metaphor, movement, imagination, feeling and involvement.

The cortex

This is your thinking brain. It is divided into two halves joined by the corpus callosum. Generally, the left side of the brain processes logic, numbers, sequential information, words and analysis. The right side processes rhythm, spatial awareness, whole pictures, imagination and dimensions. There is, however, evidence that if one side of the brain is damaged (especially in young children), the other side will take on the functions of the damaged areas.

Know your mind and environment

The more ideal your environment is for *you* to learn (everyone is different), the more effective learning will be. Unfortunately, this is not an ideal world and the likelihood of creating an entirely perfect environment for learning is small. If, however, you know what your ideal is, you will at least be able to create it in part. To learn more about your perfect learning environment, complete the following questionnaire.

Tip

The results from this or any exercise in this chapter are accurate for the present time and space. If you complete this exercise at work, you may get slightly different results than if you do it at home. Your mood and surroundings may alter the way you answer the questions. The results will provide you with *guidelines*; treat them as such.

Questionnaire: what is your perfect learning environment?

Environment: Describe your ideal environment under the following headings:

- Sound – Do you like sound or silence? If you like music, what type and how loud do you like it?
- Light – Do you prefer natural, indoor or focused lighting?
- Temperature – Do you prefer to be warm or cool? In a breeze or at a radiator?
- Body posture – Do you like to walk as you learn? Sit? Lie down?

Motivation: What drives you?

Are you driven by:

- Forward motivation – you act because there is something you want to achieve?
- Away from motivation – you act because there is something you want to avoid?
- Internal motivation – you act because you want to achieve something?
- External motivation – you act because someone else wants you to achieve something?

Sociological: Whom do you prefer to work/learn with?

List in order of preference (1 = most preferred)

- by yourself ☐
- with one other colleague ☐
- with one other friend ☐
- a group of colleagues or peers ☐
- a group of friends ☐
- other adults ☐

Physiological

- What time of day do you feel most energetic?
- What time of day do you feel least energetic?
- When do you eat your biggest meal?
- How do you feel after lunch?
- Do you like to move as you work or remain stationary?
- How much exercise do you get each day?

Your internal environment is as, if not more, important as your external environment when you learn. The next three exercises (Hemispheric mind, Sense learning and Finding the pattern) will give some of the information you need to understand how you think when you learn. When you have that information you will be able to manage your learning to ensure the process is stress free.

Hemispheric mind

The purpose of this exercise is to determine whether you are right- or left-brain dominant.

For each numbered item there are four possible choices. In column A, 1 = 'a lot' and 2 = 'somewhat'. In column B, 3 = 'somewhat' and 4 = 'a lot'. Place 'o' in the appropriate space.

For instance:

Column A	1	2	3	4	Column B
Prefer cats		o			Prefer dogs

I prefer cats 'somewhat' to dogs, but not 'a lot'.

Go through the 32 items quickly.

Column A	1	2	3	4	Column B
1 Bases decisions on facts					Bases decisions on feelings
2 Prefers structure in work settings					Prefers open-ended work settings
3 Spontaneous					Deliberate
4 Understands how pieces fit					Understands from experience
5 Tries hunches					Approaches problems logically
6 Like an athlete or artist					Like an accountant or chemist
7 Like a tax lawyer					Like a criminal lawyer
8 Neat					Sloppy
9 Process orientated					Product orientated
10 Improvising new ideas					Thoughtful, both feet on ground
11 Prefers change and the unusual					Prefers order and stability
12 Recalls information, names					Recalls faces, dress, action
13 Precise in language					Free, sweeping terms
14 Focus on words and message					Focus on body language and tone

Column A	1	2	3	4	Column B
15 Holistic intuitive					Orderly, sequential
16 Words and numbers					Space and form
17 Synthesising					Analysing
18 Abstract					Concrete
19 Emotional					Rational
20 Objective					Subjective
21 Waking					Dreaming
22 Time-bound					Timeless
23 Realistic					Idealistic
24 Led by the heart					Led by the mind
25 Specific					Ambiguous
26 Community					Agency
27 Outlook					Insight
28 Cause and effect					Resemblance
29 All at once					Bit at a time
30 Intellectual rigor					Imagination
31 Soft					Sharp
32 Persistent					Fleeting

Next, on the score sheet, circle the matching score.

	1	2	3	4
1	-2	-1	+1	+2
2	-2	-1	+1	+2
3	+2	+1	-1	-2
4	-2	-1	+1	+2
5	+2	+1	-1	-2
6	+2	+1	-1	-2
7	-2	-1	+1	+2
8	-2	-1	+1	+2
9	+2	+1	-1	-2
10	+2	+1	-1	-2
11	+2	+1	-1	-2
12	-2	-1	+1	+2
13	-2	-1	+1	+2
14	-2	-1	+1	+2
15	+2	+1	-1	-2
16	-2	-1	+1	+2
17	+2	+1	-1	-2
18	-2	-1	+1	+2
19	+2	+1	-1	-2
20	+2	+1	-1	-2
21	-2	-1	+1	+2
22	-2	-1	+1	+2
23	-2	-1	+1	+2
24	+2	+1	-1	-2
25	-2	-1	+1	+2
26	+2	+1	-1	-2
27	+2	+1	-1	-2
28	-2	-1	+1	+2
29	+2	+1	-1	-2
30	-2	-1	+1	+2
31	+2	+1	-1	-2
32	-2	-1	+1	+2

To work out your score

Total of all minus numbers you circled = ☐

Total of all plus numbers you circled = ☐

Work out the difference between the two = ☐

Results

If your score is less than –8, you are left-brain dominant.

If your score is more than +8, you are right-brain dominant.

If your score is between –8 and +8 you tend to use both hemispheres in a balanced way.

If you are extremely left- or right-brain dominant, take up activities that will balance your thinking. For instance, if you are very right-brain, practise mental arithmetic or, instead of just listening to music or looking at art, analyse it. If you are very left-brain, go to galleries and study sculpture (without trying to analyse it!)

Sense learning

Most people have a dominant sense. Determining which yours is will give you the information you need to help strengthen other senses. The more senses you use as you learn, the faster you will learn and the longer you will remember new information. The following is taken from Colin Rose's book *Accelerated Learning* (Accelerated Learning Systems Ltd. 1991).

In this exercise there are three options to choose from – A, B or C. Number each option 1 to 3 depending on which you are most prone to do:

  1 = *least* likely
  2 = sometimes
  3 = *most* likely

When you are...	Do you...
spelling	**A** see the word in your head: does it look right? **B** say it out loud: does it sound right? **C** write it out?
concentrating	**A** get distracted by untidiness? **B** get distracted by noise? **C** get distracted by movement/ physical disturbance?
choosing a favourite art form	**A** prefer paintings? **B** prefer music? **C** prefer dance/sculpture?
rewarding someone	**A** write praises to them in a note? **B** tell them? **C** give them a pat on the back?
talking	**A** talk fast, with little idle conversation, use lots of images, e.g. needle in a haystack? **B** talk fluently, logical order, few hesitations, and with clear enunciation? **C** use lots of hand movements, talk about emotions and feelings, and speak slower with pauses?
meeting people	**A** remember how they look and the surroundings? **B** remember what they said and their names? **C** remember what you did with them and your emotions?

When you are...	Do you...
watching a movie, TV or reading	**A** remember what the scenes and people looked like? **B** remember what was said and the music? **C** remember what happened and the characters' emotions?
trying to interpret someone's mood	**A** note their facial expressions? **B** listen to their tone of voice? **C** watch bodily movements?
recalling something	**A** remember what you saw, faces and how things looked? **B** remember what was said, names and jokes? **C** remember what was done and what it felt like?
memorising	**A** memorise by writing? **B** memorise by repeating? **C** memorise by doing repeatedly?
angry	**A** become silent and seethe? **B** express in an outburst? **C** storm about, clench your fists and throw things?
inactive	**A** look around, doodle and watch something? **B** talk to yourself or others? **C** fidget and walk about?

When you are...		Do you...
expressing yourself	**A**	use phrases like: I see I get the picture Let's shed some light on this
	B	use phrases like: That sounds all right I hear you! That rings a bell Something tells me It suddenly clicked
	C	use phrases like: That feels right I'm groping in the dark for answers I've got a grip on that I need a concrete example
learning	**A**	prefer to read, see the words, illustrations and diagrams?
	B	like to be told, attend lectures, talk it over?
	C	like to get involved, hands on, try it out?
assembling equipment	**A**	look at the diagrams, read the instructions?
	B	ask someone to tell you what to do, talk to yourself as you do it?
	C	work with the pieces without bothering with the instructions?

Results

To determine your dominant sense, add the totals of each letter:

Total A = ☐ Visual
Total B = ☐ Auditory
Total C = ☐ Kinaesthetic

If you are very dominant in one sense, take up activities that strengthen the other senses, for example:

Visual activities

- watch films
- read books
- visualisation
- focus on what people wear and look like
- go to galleries and enjoy the paintings

Auditory activities

- listen to music
- speak to people on the phone
- go to lectures and seminars
- focus on people's tone of voice
- pay attention to sounds around you

Kinaesthetic activities

- anything using your hands: paining, pottery
- physical activities, sport
- focus on how people make you feel
- attend dance performances
- go to galleries and enjoy the sculpture

Find the pattern

One of the greatest factors that can contribute to effective learning is your ability to identify the pattern in the structure of knowledge. It is easier to learn one new piece of information and then work out how to apply it in ten different ways, than to learn ten different pieces of information.

Counting from 1 to 99 in Japanese (in ten minutes)

English	Japanese
one	*ichi*
two	*ni*
three	*san*
four	*shi*
five	*go*
six	*roccu*
seven	*shichi*
eight	*hachi*
nine	*ku*
ten	*ju*

Before you learn how to count from one to ten in Japanese, the words mean nothing to you. The Japanese is simply a collection of sounds. To make it easier to learn, turn the sounds into something you can identify with, and turn that into an image or sensation. For example, *ichi* sounds like 'itchy' – itchy foot. So when you want to remember the Japanese for one, remember itchy foot. *Ni* sounds like 'knee'. *San* sounds like 'sun'. *Shi* sounds like 'she'... Now, instead of memorising random, meaningless sounds, you will be able to visualise clear images that represent the information.

When you have learned the basic structure, find the pattern.

English	Japanese
eleven	*ju ichi*
twelve	*ju ni*
thirteen	*ju san*
twenty	*ni ju*
twenty-one	*ni ju ichi*
twenty-two	*ni ju ni*
twenty-three	*ni ju san*
thirty	*san ju*
thirty-five	*san ju go*

Tip

11 is 10 + 1 (*ju ichi*)
20 is 2 + 10 (*ni ju*)
21 is 2 + 10 + 1 (*ni ju ichi*)

When you have found the pattern you will notice that you don't have to learn 99 different words to be able to count from 1 to 99, you only have to learn ten and understand the structure.

The same principle applies to mental arithmetic. Unless you were taught how to think mathematically, your head will probably go blank if someone were to ask you what 19 × 18 is. However, mental arithmetic is relatively easy if you look for patterns in the numbers.

19 × 18 might seem like two difficult numbers to work with. So, instead of working *that* equation out, go to the nearest round number and work from there:

20 × 20 = 400 (closest round number)
minus 20 = 380 (because the first part of the equation is 19 not 20)
minus 38 = 342 (2 × 19 where 2 comes from 20 −18)
19 × 18 = 342

Working out VAT

To work out 17.5% VAT on £100:

Determine 10% of the original figure	*10% of £100 is £10*
Divide the 10% by 2	*£10 divided by 2 is £5*
Divide that amount by 2 again	*£5 divided by 2 is £2.50*
Add the three figures together	*£10 + £5 + £2.50 = £17.50*

The VAT on £100 is £17.50

Pick an amount, and try it. Do it on paper if you want to and when you are confident that you are getting the answer right, progress to working it out mentally.

If you don't enjoy maths, then play with numbers in this way. It will:

- improve your ability to concentrate
- increase your capacity to visualise
- make you feel great when you get it right!

Ten tips on learning

1. Relax and enjoy not knowing something.
2. Know that you will get worse before you get better.
3. Make a point of learning about something you wouldn't naturally be interested in.
4. The six stages of learning are not only for learning new information. Apply the learning process to sport and physical activity as well.
5. Learn at least one new thing every day.
6. Make learning a group or family activity.
7. Challenge yourself. Every time you do something new, you expand your ability. Never say no to a new opportunity unless it's going to do you or someone else harm.
8. Don't be afraid to be wrong.
9. Ask carefully thought out questions – the better the questions, the better the answer.
10. Learn to laugh at yourself.

INSTANT TIP

Learn in a way that suits your brain and you will never be afraid to try anything new again (except maybe bungee jumping!).

10

How do you live life – not just survive day by day?

We don't dream of retiring at sixty or sixty-five anymore. We dream of stopping work at forty or fifty giving us time to do all the other things we want to do in life.

Although information can tie you down and overwhelm you, it can also set you free. As we grow into adulthood most of us develop an assumption that we know how the world works. For some, life is a struggle; living cheque to cheque, never knowing what's going to hit them next. For others, life seems easy. Instead of wondering what these people are doing differently to make life seem so easy, strugglers carry on struggling as if there's some lifelong competition to see who can bring the most tragic stories to the water cooler.

The truth is that there is no need to struggle. The better your information about how the world works is, the easier life becomes. Instead of allowing random information to clutter your mind, take the time to find out what you need to know to live an easy life.

For instance, ours is an economic society. If you're stuggling financially, chances are, you're collecting the wrong financial information. Don't put up with struggle. Learn how money works. That's information worth spending some time on.

In this chapter find the information you need to live life rather than survive it:

- Work out what you really want from life and what you need to know to make it happen.
- Plan life instead of responding to crisis.
- Put money and debt into perspective.

Financial security and dealing with debt

If your finances are in disarray, you will be distracted subconsciously – and sometimes consciously – before you even begin your daily activities, whether they are work or leisure, from when the mail arrives in the morning, through to when you pay for dinner at night. Have you ever had a feeling of doom when you offer your 'plastic'? Will it be refused? Images of the supermarket queue built up behind you, the cashier tells you the card has been declined. Run? Make an excuse? Leave? Write a cheque? Would they take a cheque? Fear, frustration, embarrassment …

Are you in the habit of ignoring your finances and hoping that somehow they will have magically put themselves in order? No news is not always good news as far as money is concerned. When the crunches (plural) come, they will not be as easy to sort as they would if you have been 'taking care of business' as you go along.

Examine the facts

Without referring to any bank or credit card statements, get a piece of paper and write on it:

1. The names of *all* debit, credit and store cards you have and:
   a. their current balance
   b. the exact date that the next payment is due on each
   c. how much will be going out of your bank account
2. All direct debits or standing orders on your bank account and:
   a. how much each is for
   b. when they are due out
3. Your bank balances and:
   a. the dates of the next income
   b. the amounts of the next income.

When you have done that, get all your latest bank, credit and store card statements. Check how accurate you were.

Could you do it? How close were you? Did you not even start because you didn't have the information in your head?

Fear about money only exists when you don't have the facts. If your finances are in order life is a whole lot easier. There is a very good reason why money is called currency – if you have it you are current. If your finances are in order you can do what you choose to do or need to do free from stress or worry.

There is only one reason why people have money problems – they spend more each month than they bring in. Gradually, the debt problem builds up to a level where the debt outweighs any possibility of paying it off so they get trapped into debt payment systems that charge massive interest and never allow them to really clear the debt fully. For those who are unfortunate enough to be in this position, their finances may look something like this:

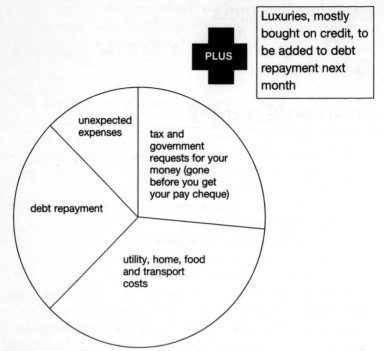

Figure 10.1 The debt trap.

The ideal scenario is that you clear your debt, reduce your tax burden, allow for unexpected expenses (for instance, vehicle repairs, dental treatment), get the best deals on your general living expenses, and learn how to make your money work for you. This chapter is not a comprehensive guide on how to get financially sorted; there are several superb books on the subject listed in the Further Reading section at the back of this book. What this chapter will do is help you clear your head about your money so you can start to clear it for real. It might give you a much needed jolt that will get you off your backside and moving towards a genuinely secure financial future.

If, after you have sorted your finances, you find you don't have any money, you will still be better off because you will know how much you don't have and you are also more likely to do something about it.

Emotional money

Do this *before* you read any further:

1. Get your wallet or purse or whatever you keep your money in.
2. Take out the note of the highest value/denomination.
3. Now, tear it in half.

Have you done it yet? Have you torn it in half? Are you still holding onto it in one piece, saying 'no chance!!'?

What are you feeling at the moment? What's going on in your mind? Are you thinking about the value of the currency you are holding and that if you tore it in half you would lose it? Or did you wait until you realised that you could tear it in half because a piece of tape would put it back in one piece again and make it money again instead of scrap paper?

If tearing that note in half was difficult, imagine what you are doing with money anyway. You might be paying an insurance policy that will be worth nothing by the time you want to cash it in (tearing money in half). Every time you buy something you never use (tearing money in half). Every time you pay more than you should for something because you can't be bothered looking for a better deal (tearing money in half).

We put a lot of emotion into money. Losing it upsets us. Not being paid enough agitates us. Being paid too much worries us. Having it makes us feel safe and secure. Not having it makes us feel frightened and 'not current'. Ironically, not having it can make us feel that we will remain part of something. How often have we heard about lottery winners losing everything within a year or a few months of winning millions? Is it because they don't know how to manage money if they've never had it before? Or is it because it's safer to be like everyone else and worry about not having enough money?

For some reason, the emotion we attach to money disappears as soon as it doesn't look like money anymore. Even credit cards manage to deceive you. Have you ever attempted to buy something to the value of £8, and at the till you are told that they only take credit cards for purchases over £10, so you pick up something you really don't need or want, to make it £10 or more. You won't have to do that often for it to have an impact on your monthly cash flow. Besides, if you were paying cash and were told that you couldn't pay cash for anything less than £10, wouldn't you walk out of the shop? Wouldn't you think you were being manipulated and ripped off? Yes, you would. But, because plastic doesn't hold the same emotional value as cash, you are happy to let yourself be ripped off!

Education

We are the way we are about money primarily because we were never taught to be any other way. We were taught how to earn money – get an education, get a job, get a better education, get a better job, the better your job the higher your salary, and so on. However, the higher your salary, the higher your taxes, the bigger your house, the greater the cost. People in one-bedroom apartments can have more disposable income than those living in penthouses whose disposable income is often disposed of before they even get it! We are not taught how to make money work and we are not taught how to generate an income unless it involves working a full week. We are not taught that living is meant for learning and exploration and expansion, growth, excitement and passion. Instead we are taught that if we have a good job, and earn a good wage, we are a success. Tosh!

There is so much more to life than just working to earn enough to pay taxes and bills. Get your money in order and get your head straight about the value of money and how to make it work. It's much more fun.

Technology is designed for personal financial management. Instead of waiting for your statements to come through once a month, you can use Internet online banking and be fully informed anytime, anywhere about your money.

Wealthy people don't just know how to make money, they know how to spend it and manage it.

Below is a strategy for getting your finances in order. You will appreciate that money is far from the 'root of all evil'. The more you know about your money, the easier it is to make more. It is merely currency; the material that society uses to allow us to exchange goods and services. The more current you are, the more freely you can interact with society at large.

Perhaps more importantly, if you understand your finances, you will be much more confident, you will be less stressed, and, each and every day, you will experience less fear.

Learn about money

Learn how to manage money. Learn how to *make* it as opposed to just earn it. Learn how to spend it and invest it. Learn how to enjoy it. Before that, learn about your current financial position.

Knowing where your money goes

Even though it might seem like a big job, this exercise may be one of the most important you will ever do. Take time out and do it. You will be surprised by what you find. The insight will allow you to manage your expenditure with your 'eyes open'.

1. Gather the last 12 months' bank, store and credit card statements (even if it costs you to get copies).
2. Either on a PC or paper, create a spreadsheet with columns breaking down exactly what goes out each month. Categorise the expenditures according to what they are, i.e. food, clothing, transport, taxes, heating, telephone or electricity bills, dinner out, entertainment, computers and technology, etc.
3. Add up each category; for instance, what you spent on clothing each month for the last year.
4. To get an average expenditure per month through the year for a particular category, divide the number for that category by 12.

Do this thoroughly and honestly. If you avoid being truthful, you will deceive only yourself.

The reason for this exercise is that although you make a purchase in one month, if you buy on credit, you pay for it for anything from six months to four years later (plus interest). This impacts your cash flow by increasing monthly debt payments and decreasing disposable income and capital.

When a friend of mine did this exercise he found that in that year he had spent an average of £6,000 per month on IT equipment (£72K in the year!) Most of this was bought on credit so the final pay-off was much higher because of very high interest! This included everything: printers, inks, consumables and any other hardware. It did not include paper. He had no idea that so much income was going towards technology that simply seemed like a good idea at the time!

When he was aware of what he was spending his money on, he was able to reduce these outgoings and manage his expenditure more intelligently.

Tearing the note in half showed you how emotionally attached you are to money. You now also have a good idea of where it goes each month.

Open your eyes and clear your mind of financial overload

Money problems are difficult to manage if you don't know what is going on. As hard as it may seem, make yourself aware of your financial situation. Get into a habit of reading and analysing your bank and credit card statements every month. Then do the following:

1. Contact your bank and get a list of all the direct debits and standing orders you have on your accounts and check all of these outgoings against the actual bills.
2. Check all of the life/death insurance policies you have. Contact the company providing them and make sure that what you are paying over time makes financial sense.
3. Check and fully understand *all* your bank charges and other fees the bank takes from your account every month. Banks do sometimes make mistakes; check that they are not over-charging you for anything.
4. Check all the purchases you made on credit. Some credit companies have higher interest rates than others. If you can, increase the payments each month or pay the 'expensive credit' off as early as you can. You will save a lot of interest.

Check and double-check

When we (*TK and MT*) moved house two years ago we didn't check all of the direct debits and found (a year later) that we had been paying the gas and electricity bill of the previous house all that time. The new owner of our home didn't complain (his bill was getting paid for him!). The utility company was getting paid, so they didn't complain. Fortunately we got it all back. We could have lost a lot of money.

5. Keep the interest payments as low as possible by moving money between cards. Check the rate of interest on your credit cards. Most companies advertise a low interest rate for the first six months. Some offer an ongoing low interest rate even after the initial six months. If you have such a card, use it to keep down your interest. Be proud to be a card tart! But also be careful because it takes considerable effort to keep your eye on the game. Moving money between 0% interest cards has a double edged benefit; not only will it keep your interest down, but finding, applying for and managing your credit in this way

Learn the facts

A colleague of mine (*MT*) recently cancelled a policy that no amount of maths could make sensible. Each month he was paying £165 into the policy. He contacted the company for a redemption figure and was quoted £704 (he had been paying into the policy for two years!). Two months later he contacted the company again for an updated figure and the value of the policy had gone up by £6. He had in the meantime paid in £130! The policy would be fully redeemable in another ten years and he would be getting (once all the fees and charges had been paid) less than what he had paid. This may be OK if the cover suits your need and you are prepared to pay for it. Investments and policies are meant to be places where your money works (e.g. you pay £1 and get back £1.50 over time). The important thing is to be aware and make informed choices. Check your investments. Don't take for granted that because some Independent Financial Advisor said it's a good deal, that it is; it's generally a good deal because the advisor gets the best commission from it. This may sound cynical, but it's reality. Learn the facts for yourself – not everyone has your best interests in mind. Be responsible for your own money.

will be so time consuming you might just find it easier to clear the lot and use that energy to invest your money rather than blow it on stuff you don't need.

6. If you automatically pay the full amount on each card every month you should pay no interest at all.

7. Since credit card companies make money from your interest payments and other charges they are often reluctant to help you completely clear the balance each month and thus pay no interest at all. If you want to arrange this, and they will not let you do it, close that account and move to a new credit card company that will. Also, don't take for granted that because you have asked the credit card company to take the full amount each month that they will. In my experience, they seem to conveniently forget instructions like that and charge you the interest anyway!

If you want to be financially literate, then keeping a record of your finances is vital. When you know exactly what your financial situation is, you will have two choices:

1. Adjust your way of life to fit your income.
2. Adjust your income to fit your way of life.

Money and guilt

Have you ever been out with a group of friends for a meal and felt compelled to pay more than your fair share? Or been in the pub and had to buy the first round, which is usually the most expensive since everyone will have one, and has the added disadvantage that the round will probably come back to you before the night is out? Have you ever bought a round and felt annoyed that as a light drinker or teetotaller your are paying for more expensive drinks for everyone else?

This social behaviour stems from our reluctance to talk about pounds and pennies. If everyone were to pay for their share they would have to discuss money. For most of us, it's easier to say, 'I'll get this' instead of 'I'll only pay for my share'.

Instead of being socially bonding this can lead to resentment and damaged friendships.

Ten tips on overload and dealing with money

1. Do not evade dealing with money issues.
2. When money is flowing well, don't get complacent.
3. Don't delay. Get cheques to the bank promptly.
4. Pay bills on time.
5. Become friendly with your bank manager and your local tax office.
6. Get a good accountant. Agree a fixed annual rate and pay in advance by standing order or direct debit. That means you can speak to them whenever you need without fearing a bill each time you ask a question.
7. Be honest with yourself about your money.
8. Avoid the vicious cycle of 'maxing out' your cards, paying them off with some 'low interest' loan and then maxing them out again.
9. It's tempting to shop around for everything. But remember to weigh the difference between the value of your time and the amount you will save by looking for a bargain.
10. Cheapest is not always best!

Starving guilt

Next time you are out in a group, say straightforwardly that you would prefer to pay for your own meal instead of an equal share. You can be diplomatic. Say that you might want something more expensive and don't want others to subsidise you. That allows you to choose what you want, enjoy your meal, stick to your budget and keep your friends.

When someone in a group offers to buy a round, thank them and tell them that you prefer to get your own. That will take you out of the 'loop'.

It won't be easy. There will be pressure to conform. But if you want to get a grip on your money, begin by not letting others spend it for you.

In dealing with money, you will make mistakes. When something goes wrong and it costs you, instead of getting angry, frustrated and fearful that it will happen again, learn from it. Provided you *do* learn from the situation, treat the cost as 'school fees' – paying for an education.

Information overload in a busy world

A successful and proven method of managing non-fiction material is the five-step reading strategy outlined in Chapter 5. If you need to refresh your memory, go back to Chapter 5 and re-read it. In addition to the five-step strategy, there are a number of other techniques you can use to help minimise the unwanted information you are presented with.

Information has the potential to instil terror in the boldest souls: 'If I don't read this/understand this/know this, what will I be missing and what will the consequences be?'

Most of the seemingly infinite information to which you have access to is irrelevant to your purposes. Overloading with 'non-sense' contributes greatly to mental block and overload. I can't overemphasise how important it is to identify, then ignore, irrelevant information.

You are exposed to this risk much more so if you work in a large organisation. If you want your desk and your mind to remain clear, develop your ability to identify and prioritise relevance. This will help prevent clutter in your mental and physical spaces and put a barrier up against overload. I say 'put a barrier up' because with every piece of information you are given a choice: accept it, do something with it, attach a consequence to it, add it to your 'maybe later' pile or ditch it.

Choices we make that lead to overload

The 'need to know everything' syndrome will turn your desk into an information bottleneck and take up a huge proportion of your mental and physical time, unnecessarily. Some symptoms and their 'cures' are outlined here:

Apparent urgency: dealing with something as soon as you receive it no matter what else has to be done or how important it really is. If someone gives you a document to read and says, 'This is urgent, you must read it now', don't take their word for it. It may be urgent to them. In your day it might come second or fifteenth. Prioritise all new work and interruptions. Stay on purpose.

Nobody does it better: excellent attitude if you want to work every weekend and most holidays. Most people are capable of doing their jobs well. Think lucky, have faith, prioritise and delegate.

Generosity: when it comes to your own time you cannot always afford to be generous. Often the people giving you something extra to deal with are trying to avoid doing what they have been tasked with. Distinguish between being 'delegated to' versus being 'dumped on'!

Don't accept every piece of information that lands on your desk without establishing:

1. that you are the best person to process the information
2. why you should read it
3. what you are expected to do with it.

Prioritise information

The more effectively you prioritise your reading the faster you will get through it. You will be surprised at how much you can achieve when you enlist the help of others and share information. When unread material piles so high that you feel you can't do anything about it, you will experience a feeling of exhaustion when you approach your desk, commonly known as 'paper fatigue'.

When you prioritise, you are much less likely to become an information bottleneck. If you are starting with a large quantity of unprioritised documents this might take some time. Do it once however, and you will get used to prioritising and will do it naturally on a daily basis.

To prioritise effectively:

1. Gather all your backlogged reading or paperwork.
2. Sort it into groups:
   a. **Urgent:** if you don't deal with/read this, something, somewhere will go drastically wrong – soon.
   b. **Important:** if you don't deal with/read this now, the world won't collapse, but if you leave it too long, it might.
   c. **Useful:** information that would be good to know, but is not urgent.
   d. **Nice to know:** information that is nice have access to, but if you never read it, it wouldn't matter. This might include magazine and newspaper articles you thought looked interesting.
   e. **Bin:** bin!
3. Go through each pile, starting with the 'urgent' pile, sort it into **pay-off** or **rip-off**. Will the document make you money (give you value) or cost you money if you do not deal with it? If any documents in the 'urgent' pile do not have a pay-off, perhaps they are not so urgent. Also consider whether they are 'urgent' because someone else said so?
4. Quickly determine how long each document will take to read. Plan the reading into your day according to when you will need the information. Reading something that you will not use for several weeks will mean that you will have to revise it. Date it and read it when it is necessary (sometimes procrastinating is the right thing to do).

If you consistently receive documents that you don't need, it can be annoying and time-wasting. Receiving as little 'junk mail' as possible will help make daily prioritisation much easier.

How to reduce your junk mail intake

1. Collect all reports, journals, documents and memos that require your attention.

2. To establish any patterns ask these questions: Does the same person or office consistently send irrelevant material? Is it vital to your job? Have you any interest in the subject matter? Do they arrive regularly without you asking for them? Have you requested them? If so, for what purpose?

3. When you have established which documents are useful to you, briefly study each one. Is it written such that you can gather information without reading the whole document? How long would it take to read the summaries and conclusions? Would it be sufficient? If you don't need to read the whole document, does the person who wrote it know? If you only receive what you need, you could both save time.

4. Determine the actions required to take the issues arising from the documents forward. If most of the reports and memos are 'for information only' and you don't have actions arising from them, their urgency and importance will diminish.

5. Could you get the information by speaking to someone? Perhaps under the guise of socialising for a few minutes.

6. Is the information still valid by the time you receive it? Or is it old news?

7. If you are not clear about whether you have to read something, put it aside as a test. If someone asks you to act on it, you may have to pay attention to it in the future.

When you have categorised the material, prioritise it as discussed earlier. If you don't need the reports or memos, ask to be excluded from the mailing list.

In brief

1. Have your purpose clearly in mind when you review any information.
2. Set a time limit for how long you will spend on dealing with information.
3. When dealing with mail make the bin the preferred option.
4. Deal with 'incoming' information as quickly as possible.
5. Keep your desk clear of everything except your current project.
6. Do unto others ... don't send junk mail to other people.
7. If you have a filing system, make it work for you by helping you find information efficiently.
8. Don't assume that others either know or want to know everything you do.
9. Good questions render good information. Think of the kind of answers you want when you ask questions.
10. Don't just store information, use it.

Some time ago I met a doctor who was taking some teasing over his time management system: it consisted of a scrappy piece of paper curled up in his pocket that only got binned when it became illegible or got caught in the wash. His friends were comparing his system to 'how it should be done'. He took it in good humour then said, 'It doesn't matter what it looks like, it works'.

The same is true of information overload. It doesn't matter what system you use. If it works, then it works. There are a considerable number of strategies in this book. Pick what works for you, clear the decks and get on with your glorious life.

INSTANT TIP

Don't be afraid of the difficult things in life. Face them head on. Deal with them. Win. Move on.

Further reading

Beaver, Diane (1994) *Lazy Learning*, Element

Berger, David (2000) *The Motley Fool UK Investment Guide*, Boxtree

Berry, Cicely (1994) *Your Voice and How to Use it Successfully*, Virgin Books

Decker, Bert (1989) *How to Communicate Effectively*, Kogan Page

Denny, Richard (1994) *Speak for Yourself*, Kogan Page

de Porter, Bobby and Hernacki, Mike (1995) *Quantum Learning*, Piatkus Books

Cava, Roberta (1999) *Dealing with difficult people*, Piatkus Books

Cialdini, Robert (2000) *Influence: Practice and Science*, Addison-Wesley Education Publishers

Conradi and Hall, (2001) *That Presentation Sensation*, Financial Times Prentice Hall

Dilts, Robert B. (1994) *Effective Presentation Skills*, Meta Publications inc.

Dryden, Gordon and Vos, Jeanette (1994) *The Learning Revolution*, Accelerated Learning Systems Ltd.

Dudley, Geoffrey A. (1986) *Double your Learning Power*, Thorsons

Fisher, Roger (1997) *Getting to Yes*, Arrow

Forsyth, Patrick (1995) *Making Successful Presentations*, Sheldon

Furst, Bruno (1987) *The Practical Way to a Better Memory*, R&W Heap Publishing

Grant and Greene, (2001) *Coach Yourself*, Momentum

Grove, David (1989) *Resolving Traumatic Memories: Metaphors and Symbols in Pyschotherapy*, Irvington Publishers

Herrmann, Raybeck and Gutman (1996) *Improving Student Memory*, Hogrefe & Huber Publishers

Hooper, Judith and Teresi, Dick (1992) *The Three Pound Universe*, Tarcher Putnam

Hunt, D. Trinidad (1993) *Learning to Learn*, Elan

Jay, (2001) *Fast Thinking Presentation*, Prentice Hall

Jay, (2001) *Fast Thinking Managers Manual*, Prentice Hall

Khalsa, Dr Dharma Singh (1997) *Brain Longevity*, Century

Kiyosaki, Robert T. (1998) *Rich Dad, Poor Dad*, Warner Business Books

Kiyosaki, Robert T. (2001) *Rich Dad, Poor Dad's Guide to Investing*, Warner Business Books

Konstant, Tina (2007) *Speed-reading in a Week*, Hodder and Stoughton

Konstant, Tina (2007) *Teach Yourself Speed-reading*, Hodder and Stoughton

Lorayne, Harry and Lucas, Jerry (1974) *The Memory Book*, Dorset Press

Luria, (1968) *The Mind of a Mnemonist*, Harvard

Markham, Ursula (1993) *Memory Power*, Vermillion

McConnell, (2001) *Change Activist*, Momentum

Michalko, Michael (2001) *Cracking Creativity: The Secrets of Creative Genius*, Ten Speed Press

Mirsky, Nick (1994) *The Unforgettable Memory Book*, BBC

Morrison, Malcome (2001) *Clear Speech*, A & C Black

O'Connor and Seymour, (1994) *Training with NLP*, HarperCollins

Ostrander, Sheila and Schroeder, Lynn (1992) *Cosmic Memory*, Simon and Schuster

Ostrander, Sheila and Schroeder, Lynn (1994) *Superlearning 2000*, Souvenir Press

Rose, Colin (1991) *Accelerated Learning*, Accelerated Learning
    Systems Ltd.
Rossi, Ernest (1991) *The 20 Minute Break*, Jeremy P. Tarcher
Rossi, Ernest (1994) *Psychobiology of Mind Body Healing*,
    W. W. Norton
Schwartz, David J. (1986) *Maximise Your Mental Power*, Thorsons
Smith, Manual J. (1975) *When I Say No I Feel Guilty*,
    Bantam Press
Szantesson, Ingemar (1994) *Mind Mapping and Memory*,
    Kogan Page
Tame, David (1984) *The Secret Power of Music*, Destiny Books
Templar (2001) *Fast Thinking Difficult People*, Prentice Hall
Templar (2001) *Fast Thinking Work Overload*, Prentice Hall
Ury, William (1992) *Getting Past No*, Random House
Yates, Frances A. (1974) *The Art of Memory*, Pimlico

Index